# RUSSIA AND THE USSR 1905–1991

Philip Ingram

CAMBRIDGE
UNIVERSITY PRESS

**For Jimmy and Holly**

PUBLISHED BY THE PRESS SYNDICATE OF THE UNIVERSITY OF CAMBRIDGE
The Pitt Building, Trumpington Street, Cambridge CB2 1RP, United Kingdom

CAMBRIDGE UNIVERSITY PRESS
The Edinburgh Building, Cambridge CB2 2RU, United Kingdom
40 West 20th Street, New York, NY 10011–4211, USA
10 Stamford Road, Oakleigh, Melbourne 3166, Australia

© Cambridge University Press 1997

First published 1997

Printed in the United Kingdom at the University Press, Cambridge

Typeset in Octavian and Meta

*A catalogue record for this book is available from the British Library*

*Library of Congress cataloguing in publication data applied for*

ISBN 0 521 56867 6 paperback

Produced by Gecko Limited, Bicester, Oxon

Illustrations by Gecko Limited, Bicester, Oxon

Picture research by Marilyn Rawlings

**Acknowledgements**
Cover, David King; 4*l*, 9, 18, 20, Novosti, London; 4*r*, 5, 6, 8, 10, 11, 13, 15, 16 (background), 17, 21, 24*l* 24*r*, 26, 27, 31 (background), 32, 33, 34, 35, 37*t*, 37*b*, 39, 40, 44*t*, 44*bl*, 44*br*, 46 (background), 47, 48*l*, 50, 51, 52*t*, 52*b*, 53, 54 (background), 56, 57, 58, David King; 7, 30, Hulton Getty; 12, 19, Mansell Collection; 38, Fotomas Index; 41, AKG, London; 45, International Institute of Social History, Amsterdam; 48*r*, Network; 55, Ullstein Bilderdienst; 59, 60*t*, Topham; 60*b*, 62 (background), Sipa-Press, Paris; 61, Popperfoto.

# Contents

# Russia's problems under Tsar Nicholas II

In 1900, Russia was a huge empire of many different peoples. It was held together by one man, Nicholas II, known as the Tsar (emperor). His family, the Romanovs, had ruled the country for around three hundred years. Most of his subjects were peasants, although the number of industrial workers was increasing. He had a largely loyal population, growing industrial wealth and complete power. It might seem that he had no real problems to face. Yet, despite his wealth and power, he was faced with difficult choices.

## Could the Tsar solve Russia's problems?

### The problems of the countryside

Russian peasants were desperately poor. The population was increasing and there did not seem to be enough land to provide for them all. Their problems were made much worse by inefficient farming methods. Farming was organised on a village basis by the mir (village council). Individual peasants could not act on their own to improve farming techniques without the support of the mir.

Most peasants were loyal to the Tsar and the Romanov family. They did not blame their beloved Tsar for their poverty. Instead they criticised the nobles who, they felt, had cheated them of land that rightly belonged to them. From 1900 onwards, a series of violent disturbances broke out in many country areas. Land belonging to the nobles was seized and occupied by the peasants. This was not a direct threat to the Tsar, but both nobles and peasants looked to him for a solution.

**SOURCE B**

A peasant family in the doorway of their small wooden shack.

**SOURCE A**

A nobleman's family, with a number of peasants who work on their estate, at their house near Moscow.

As the Tsar needed the support of the nobles, he could not be seen to side with the peasants. At the same time, he had to find some way to calm their anger and make farming more productive. His Chief Minister, Peter Stolypin (1906–11), introduced reforms that allowed peasants to set up their own farms, outside the control of the mir. He hoped that improved farming methods would increase the numbers of prosperous, independent peasants known as kulaks. The kulaks would then be able to pay more tax to the government and would help make the countryside peaceful. By 1914 his policy had achieved only limited success and 90 per cent of all peasants still remained under the control of the mirs. Many hungry peasants moved to the cities to find work.

## The problems of the cities

Under Sergei Witte (Minister of Finance 1890–1903), Russian industry grew very quickly. Witte encouraged foreign investment and built thousands of kilometres of railways. Industrial workers had hard lives. They suffered long hours and dangerous conditions for very low pay. The speed of industrialisation led to overcrowding in the cities. Many slept in their factories, others lived in uncomfortable barracks, and even those fortunate enough to find a flat or a room often had to share with several other families.

## SOURCE D
### Strikes in Russia 1910–14

| 1910 | 222 |
| 1911 | 466 |
| 1912 | 2032 |
| 1913 | 2404 |
| 1914 (up to July) | 4098 |

Most factory workers were unhappy. As they had no political power, they showed their discontent in frequent strikes. There were limits to how far the Tsar could help the workers. Many Russian factories were owned by foreign companies who had deliberately invested in Russia because it cost so little to employ Russian workers. If the Tsar were to pass laws forcing these companies to pay higher wages and provide better conditions, it might make the investors withdraw their money altogether. This would have wrecked the entire process of industrialisation. Some of the larger factories were owned by the Russian government but, even here, the Tsar could do little. These factories were built by borrowing money from abroad, so the government was deeply in debt. Once the government had met the huge repayments on these foreign loans, it had little money left to put towards helping the workers.

## SOURCE C

*Factory workers eating in a canteen.*

5

## Why did Russia need industry?

The Russian government wanted factories so that Russia could become rich and powerful like Britain, the USA and Germany. All these other countries had been through an industrial revolution.

Industry was also needed to strengthen Russia's ability to defend herself. Increasingly, success in war meant having the industries to supply large armies. Russia's industrial backwardness had contributed to her defeat by Britain and France in the Crimean War (1854–6). In the period after 1900, European countries began an arms race, relying on their industries to make more and more weapons. The only way for Russia to survive this threat seemed to be to make as many weapons as her enemies. This meant industrialising as quickly as possible. Whatever its cost, industrialisation had to go ahead. The scale of industrial expansion in Russia was remarkable.

### SOURCE E

By 1913, Russia was the world's second biggest oil producer but these rigs in the Baku oil fields were owned by a Swedish industrialist.

### SOURCE F

**Russian and German industrialisation in 1913**

|  | Germany | Russia |
|---|---|---|
| Coal (millions of tonnes) | 190.0 | 36.0 |
| Pig iron (millions of tonnes) | 6.8 | 4.6 |
| Steel (millions of tonnes) | 8.3 | 4.8 |
| Railways (thousands of kilometres) | 64.0 | 65.0 |

### SOURCE G

*A historian has commented on the speed with which Russia increased industrial production at this time:*

A recent Soviet textbook, which is not likely to overestimate the achievements of Tsarism, has put forward the following estimates: during the period 1860–1910 the world's industrial production increased by [a factor of] 6, Great Britain's by 2.5, Germany's by 6 and Russia's by 10.5.

Alec Nove, *An Economic History of the USSR*, 1969

## >> Activity

1. Explain the following terms:
   > Tsar
   > mir
   > kulak.

2. Why was there unrest and unhappiness in:
   > the Russian countryside;
   > the Russian cities?

3. Who were Peter Stolypin and Sergei Witte? What did each man do to develop the economy?

4. Using the whole of this unit for information, explain why Tsar Nicholas II faced huge problems in governing Russia.

# The Tsar's opponents and supporters

## Who opposed the Tsar?

There were three main political groups who opposed the Tsar.

*The Kadets* (the Constitutional Democrats) were a middle-class liberal party that wanted peaceful political change leading to the handover of power to an elected duma (parliament). Their support was restricted to the small, well-educated and wealthy population of the towns. Their programme of political reform offered nothing to attract the support of the peasants and workers. They were divided between those who were willing to work with the Tsar and those who thought that Russia must become a republic.

*The Social Revolutionaries* (the SRs) had support among a small section of the peasantry and favoured seizing power by revolution. Once in power, they would change the system of land ownership to make life better for the peasants. Although their potential support seemed huge, the very size of the country and the ignorance of the peasantry made it impossible to organise a mass movement. The Social Revolutionaries were divided in both their aims and their methods. Some simply wanted to share out the land among the peasants. Others wanted to abolish private ownership altogether and introduce a system where all land was owned by the entire community. Some wanted to achieve this by peaceful change, while others believed in using violence.

*The Social Democrats* were supported by many factory workers. They followed the communist teachings of Karl Marx (1818–83), a German writer who believed that modern industrial societies were divided between the workers (the proletariat) and the wealthy factory owners (the capitalists). Marx said that capitalists exploited the workers unfairly with the support of the government. The only way to change the situation was for the workers in every country to unite and overthrow their governments by revolution. Once the existing governments were overthrown, the proletariat would take over and introduce a true communist system, where all wealth is shared evenly and where the factories are run for the benefit of the proletariat.

In 1903, the Social Democrats split into two separate groups or factions: the Mensheviks and the Bolsheviks. The split was largely the result of an argument over how the party should gain power. The Mensheviks wanted to try to win the support of sympathetic middle-class people in order to create a political party with widespread support. They would then work gradually towards a communist society. The Bolsheviks believed that the Tsar would make it impossible to organise a mass movement like this. They thought it would be better to remain as a comparatively small group of revolutionaries, who could plot in secret and stage a revolution as soon as possible.

*An artist's impression of the assassination of the Tsar's uncle, the Grand Duke Sergei, in 1905.*
> *Which political group do you think was most likely to have been responsible for his murder?*

The split of 1903 meant that there were two rival factions in the small Social Democratic party. The members were divided in their attitude to the middle class, and had little appeal for the peasantry who made up the vast majority of the population.

## Who supported the Tsar?

The Tsar's most faithful supporters were the nobles, but he was also popular with many of the wealthiest middle-class people. They were making a good living out of the industry that he was introducing into the country. Some of them had invested in the new factories and were grateful to him for keeping the workers under control. Many peasants also supported him because the Church taught them that loyalty to the Tsar and loyalty to God were the same thing. Even those peasants and workers who did complain rarely blamed the Tsar directly. Instead, they attacked the noble landlords or the factory owners, and preferred to believe that the Tsar was a good man who was misled by bad advisers.

## The Tsar's response to opposition

The Tsar could be completely ruthless towards the people who did protest. On many occasions he used the army to put down street demonstrations with brutal force. Even those who did not protest openly but plotted in secret had little chance, for the Tsar had a highly effective, secret police force, known as the Okhrana, which spied on every area of Russian life. They could usually arrest troublemakers before any trouble occurred. Once arrested, the suspect could be tortured, imprisoned, or sent into exile in a remote part of the country. The work of the Okhrana kept illegal opposition groups weak and disorganised. By the early 1900s most of their leaders had fled abroad where they had little influence.

### THE TSAR'S OPPONENTS AND SUPPORTERS

| Against the Tsar | For the Tsar |
| --- | --- |
| The Kadets | The nobles |
| The Social Revolutionaries | The Church |
| The Social Democrats | The wealthy middle class |
| (after 1903, the Bolsheviks and the Mensheviks) | Many peasants and workers who were traditionally loyal to the Tsar |

### Discussion point

> Consider the strengths and weaknesses of each of the three opposition groups. Explain which one you think was the greatest danger to the Tsar.

A political prisoner is put in chains by the guards on Sakhalin Island, a harsh and desolate prison colony off the east coast of Russia.

# The events of 1905

### The Russo-Japanese War

Early in 1904, Russia became involved in a war with Japan over control of Manchuria and Korea. The Tsar and his ministers believed that they could achieve a quick victory that would increase their popularity at home. However, the Pacific Fleet was smashed by the Japanese at Port Arthur and, in early 1905, the Russian army was heavily defeated at Mukden. The Baltic Fleet sailed to the rescue but was, in turn, destroyed at the Battle of Tsushima. The Tsar now had to take the blame for these shocking defeats.

### The 1905 Revolution

The war caused enormous disruption to the economy. In particular, the railway system was used to keep the army supplied in the Far East. In the cities, the resulting lack of transport led to food shortages and price rises. The situation became worse when factories, which were unable to obtain raw materials, either had to lay off workers, or close down altogether. At first the workers were prepared to support the war effort, but as they became more and more desperate, and news of the defeats came in, their mood changed. They responded with a series of strikes, demanding not only higher wages, but also the right to form trade unions and have unpopular laws abolished.

*Troops firing at demonstrators outside the Winter Palace in January 1905. For many years after the event, Bloody Sunday was a favourite subject for artists.*
**>** *Why do you think this was so?*

---

**TROTSKY (1879–1940)** – (1982)

Trotsky had always been active in revolutionary politics. In 1898 he was arrested for being a Marxist and exiled to Siberia. He escaped in 1902 and spent many years abroad, hiding from the Tsarist police. He returned to Russia after the outbreak of the 1905 Revolution and became Chairman of the St Petersburg Soviet. After the Revolution failed, he was sentenced to a long term of imprisonment in Siberia. He escaped to the West and spent his time working as a political journalist. Once the Tsar had been overthrown in March 1917, he would return to St Petersburg (now renamed Petrograd).

---

On 22 January 1905, a priest named Father Gapon led 200,000 peaceful workers in a march on the Tsar's Winter Palace in St Petersburg to present a petition. The soldiers guarding the palace fired on the marchers, killing hundreds, and the incident quickly became known as 'Bloody Sunday'. Millions of workers all over Russia joined a general strike that soon paralysed the entire country. Moderates lost support for their peaceful approach, and some Social Democrats like Leon Trotsky angrily demanded a workers' government. In St Petersburg, and many other major cities, the workers organised themselves into soviets (councils) to lead the new wave of protests. Trotsky became Chairman of the St Petersburg Soviet a few weeks before it was suppressed. He managed to persuade the Mensheviks and Bolsheviks to co-operate with each other, and even put forward ambitious plans for them to re-unite.

There was also widespread unrest in the countryside. The Tsar even seemed to be losing control of the military when, in June 1905, the members of the crew of the battleship *Potemkin* mutinied and murdered their officers.

### Discussion point

> Why do you think the 1905 Revolution broke out?

# 1905 – the aftermath

In 1905 Nicholas seemed doomed. He had lost control of the cities to the workers' soviets and the countryside was in chaos. Even the army now appeared unreliable. Remarkably he managed to cling on to power.

## How did the Tsar survive the 1905 Revolution?

### Concessions

The Tsar's Chief Minister, Sergei Witte (1905–6), realised that the alliance between middle-class protesters and working-class revolutionaries could be broken. The middle class, in particular, feared the growing influence of Trotsky and the Social Democrats and opposed their demand for an eight-hour working day in the factories. At the end of 1905, Witte persuaded the Tsar to issue the 'October Manifesto', a series of laws that allowed greater freedom to the individual, and to call a duma (parliament) which would share power with the Tsar. These concessions brought middle-class opposition to an end.

### Force

The Social Revolutionaries and the Social Democrats saw that the October Manifesto offered little for the workers or peasants. They decided to continue the revolution. The Tsar employed the army to suppress all disturbances, while his Chief Minister, Stolypin (who replaced Witte in 1906), used the police and the law courts against suspected agitators. They were either hung, or sent into exile for long periods in remote areas of Russia like Siberia. Trotsky was arrested and, within a few months, the striking workers had been starved back to work and their leaders were either in prison or on the run. Order was not restored so easily in Moscow, where an armed rising by 2,000 workers was only suppressed after ten days of street fighting. In the countryside, Stolypin encouraged Tsarist gangs known as Black Hundreds to kill any peasant suspected of causing trouble.

### The duma is kept in check

The Tsar had only allowed a duma to meet in order to silence middle-class opposition, while he dealt with the workers and peasants. By 1906, he felt that it was safe to destroy the influence of the duma. He made two important additions to the reforms in his October Manifesto. He claimed the right to dismiss any duma that he did not like, and to decide how the new duma members were elected. Within a year, he had dismissed two dumas and changed the election rules so that only the very rich had a real say in elections. This meant that the next two dumas were filled with his own aristocratic supporters, who caused him no trouble.

**SOURCE A**

A later painting of the street fighting in Moscow during December 1905.
> What can you tell about the social class of the fighters?

## SOURCE B

*The Tsar stated his reasons for closing down the first duma in July 1906:*

A cruel disappointment has befallen Our expectations. The representatives of the nation, instead of applying themselves to the work of productive legislation, have strayed into spheres beyond their competence, and have been making enquiries into the acts of local authorities established by Ourselves which can only be modified by Our imperial will.

## Peace with Japan

Once Nicholas II realised that his armies were defeated, he ended the war in order to concentrate on his domestic problems. As soon as he pulled Russia out of the war, the problems that it had caused to industry began to ease, and working-class discontent was reduced. His army remained loyal throughout, and he was able to use the returning troops against those workers and peasants who still opposed him. Lastly, he skilfully exploited the divisions between his opponents, who were never able to work together. His October Manifesto split the middle class from the workers and peasants, and bought him vital time.

## The cost of the 1905 Revolution

Historians still argue about whether the failure of the 1905 Revolution meant that the Tsar was secure, or whether it merely bought him time before he was finally overthrown because of his failure to cope with Russia's problems. Stolypin believed that the regime could be saved if it could avoid war for another twenty years, but others thought that the events of 1905 left the Tsar's government doomed. His image as a caring father to his people was shattered by 'Bloody Sunday' and the brutal actions of Stolypin and the Black Hundreds. Many middle-class politicians felt that they had been tricked by the way he had treated the duma and they were determined not to trust him again. Although he had retained power, it seemed that he had lost much of the trust and affection of his people.

## SOURCE C

*Tsarist officials preparing to decorate the Imperial Palace with skulls. This Russian cartoon shows the extent to which the Tsar had lost the confidence of his subjects.*

## SOURCE D

*In 1906, the American Consul in Odessa commented on how the reaction of the Tsar and his government to the 1905 Revolution had affected their popularity.*

All classes condemn the authorities and more particularly the emperor [Tsar]. The present ruler has lost absolutely the love of the Russian people; whatever the future may have in store for the dynasty, the present Tsar will never again be safe in the midst of his people.

## >> Activity

1 What was the October Manifesto? How did it help the Tsar to stay in power?

2 How did the Tsar use brutality and repression to stay in power?

3 Why did Nicholas reduce the power of the duma in 1906?

4 Why did many Russians feel bitterness towards Tsar Nicholas II after the 1905 Revolution?

# The First World War

The First World War was a disaster for Russia. Many Russians laid all the blame on the Tsar and came to see his overthrow as the only way to save the country from a crushing defeat.

## How did the First World War help to destroy the Tsar?

### WHY WAS RUSSIA LOSING THE WAR?

With a huge army of 6 million men, it seemed that Russia could not lose. However, it proved impossible to supply this army from Russia's small industrial base. This problem was made worse by the gross inefficiency and corruption of the Tsar's administrators leading to chronic waste and confusion. The transport system was unable to carry sufficient supplies both to the towns and to the army. The army used outdated tactics and its generals were poor leaders.

### RUSSIA IN THE FIRST WORLD WAR

| | |
|---|---|
| **August 1914:** | Russia declared war on Germany and Austria–Hungary. |
| **August – September 1914:** | The Russian army was victorious against Austria at Lemberg, but was overwhelmingly defeated by Germany at the battles of Tannenberg and the Masurian Lakes. There were over a million Russian casualties. |
| **1915:** | The German army advanced deep into Russia, taking thousands of square kilometres of Russian territory. |
| **1916:** | The Russians launched the 'Brusilov Offensive' against Austria. General Brusilov's army recaptured some land but was eventually pushed back. A further million Russians were killed or wounded. |
| **1917:** | The Russian army was demoralised and nearing collapse. |

**SOURCE A**

*A Russian postcard issued in May 1916 that shows the Tsar as Commander-in-Chief.*

### FACTOR 1
### THE TSAR AS COMMANDER-IN-CHIEF

In 1915 the Tsar took overall command of the conduct of the war. This was a terrible mistake, as it meant that he could no longer blame the defeats on his subordinates but had to take all the responsibility himself. The support of the army ebbed away, as his soldiers now blamed him directly for their misery and for the high casualties. The peasants, who provided most of the army's recruits, had their image of a wise and caring Tsar further shattered by the experience of war.

## FACTOR 2
## THE TSARINA

While the Tsar was at the front, he left the running of the country in the hands of his wife, the Tsarina. She refused to take any advice from loyal middle-class members of the duma and preferred to rule herself. Her refusal to share policy decisions, just like the Tsar, meant that she came to be blamed for everything that went wrong. The patriotic middle class became more and more frustrated at the incompetence of the Tsarina and her refusal to allow them a share in government. They were convinced that they could do better.

During the war, Russian people came to hate all things German. They even changed the name of their capital city to Petrograd because St Petersburg sounded too German. The Tsarina was German. This added greatly to her unpopularity. Rumours soon spread that she was trying to sabotage Russia's war effort in order to ensure a German victory.

## FACTOR 3
## RASPUTIN

The one person the Tsarina was willing to listen to was a mysterious holy man named Rasputin. His influence over her came from his seemingly miraculous ability to heal her sick son, but his character and the many scandals that surrounded him made the Tsarina even more unpopular. Wild rumours circulated that they were both German agents. Some people were even willing to believe that Rasputin had a satanic hold over the entire royal family, and was leading the country to its doom. In December 1916, Rasputin was murdered by a group of jealous noblemen but, by then, it was too late to restore the reputation of the royal family.

## >> Activity

1  Look at the the Tsar and Tsarina in Source B. What does it tell us about attitudes towards them?

2  Look at Source C. What does it tell us about the popularity of the war in 1914?

3  Look at all of the information in this unit. Explain why the workers in towns, the peasants and the middle class all became disillusioned with the Tsar.

**SOURCE B**

*A cartoon of Rasputin with the Tsar and Tsarina. The artist emphasises Rasputin's power by showing him as a large figure in the centre of the picture.*

## FACTOR 4
## THE CRISIS IN THE CITIES

Throughout much of the war, Russian cities suffered from a shortage of food. This was due to a combination of bad harvests, poor transport arrangements and the loss of large areas of rich farmland to the Germans. The shortage meant that food prices went up by around 700 per cent during three years of war, and although workers' wages increased by 200 per cent during the same period, they did not keep pace with inflation. By the beginning of 1917, urban workers were faced with starvation.

**SOURCE C**

*A secret Petrograd Police Report, dated October 1916, described the effect of the war on the population:*

Military defeats brought the masses to a clearer understanding of war – unfair distribution of foodstuffs, an immense and rapid increase in the cost of living, an inadequacy in sources of supply. Everywhere there are exceptional feelings of hostility and opposition to the government because of the unbearable burden of the war and the impossible conditions of everyday life.

# The March 1917 Revolution

The enormous loss of confidence and support that the Tsar suffered as a result of the First World War made his government very unstable. With so little support it is hardly surprising that he was overthrown. Yet he had managed to survive such crises in the past. Why was 1917 to be so different?

## Why was the March 1917 Revolution successful?

### How was the Tsar overthrown?

In March 1917, the food shortages led to widespread looting in Petrograd. The looters were joined by thousands of striking workers in a series of violent protests. The local army garrison was called out and although some soldiers obeyed orders and fired on the rioters, many others mutinied and joined the protesting crowds. Most of the police simply stood by and refused to do anything. No major revolutionaries were involved in the March Revolution. Most of them were either in prison or in exile.

### SOURCE A

A middle-class baker enthusiastically joins the revolution. He is trampling on his shop sign which reads, 'By Appointment to the Tsar'.
> How does the cartoonist make us question the man's sincerity?

### SOURCE B

*A Bolshevik eyewitness to the soldiers' mutiny of March 1917 later stated:*

The tips of the bayonets were touching the breasts of the first row of demonstrators. Behind could be heard the singing of revolutionary songs, in front there was confusion. Women, with tears in their eyes, were crying out to the soldiers, 'Comrades, take away your bayonets, join us!' The soldiers moved. They threw swift glances at their own comrades. The next moment one bayonet is slowly raised; there is thunderous applause. The triumphant crowd greeted their brothers clothed in the grey cloaks of the soldiery. The soldiers mixed freely with the demonstrators.

In defiance of the Tsar's orders, a group of middle-class duma members met and called themselves the Provisional (temporary) Government. They intended to rule the country until proper elections could be held for a new Russian parliament. At the same time, representatives of the workers and soldiers met and re-formed the Petrograd Soviet, which had been suppressed after the 1905 Revolution. The Tsar finally realised that he had no supporters (he was even deserted by his personal bodyguard) and, in March 1917, was forced to abdicate, after failing to persuade his brother Michael to take the throne. Russia became a republic with no legal government and two rival political institutions.

## The March Revolution: planned or spontaneous?

Historians have often questioned whether the March Revolution was a planned conspiracy or whether it happened in an unplanned, spontaneous way. Most have concluded that the revolution was not planned. The Tsarist government seems to have collapsed because of its own weakness and the problems caused by the war. The Bolsheviks were not very active in the revolution. At the time, the Bolsheviks only had 25,000 members and their leader, Lenin, was far away in exile. He was completely taken by surprise by the news from Petrograd.

### SOURCE C

*Speaking in January 1917, from Zurich where he was living in exile, Lenin said that he did not expect to see a revolution in his lifetime:*

We of the older generation may not live to see the decisive battles of the coming revolution.

### SOURCE D

*A Tsarist minister, Kokovtsov, later claimed that everyone was surprised by the revolution:*

When other people say that they foresaw the revolution they are telling a complete lie. Everybody expected some political reform that would paralyse the influence of the Tsarina and set up a new administration.

### SOURCE E

---

### LENIN 1870–1924

In 1897, Lenin was exiled to Siberia for three years because of his revolutionary activities against the Tsar's government. From 1900, he lived mostly in Western Europe. After the Social Democratic Party split into two factions in 1903, he became the leader of the Bolsheviks. He wrote many political books while in exile. After the fall of the Tsar, he returned to Russia from Switzerland, arriving in Petrograd in April 1917, where he was soon joined by Trotsky.

---

## >> Activity

1  Look at Source B. What does it tell us about the attitude of the soldiers? Explain why this was significant.

2  Using all the information in this unit, explain how important a role the Bolsheviks played in the March 1917 Revolution.

*Lenin, in 1920, reading a copy of the newspaper* Pravda.

# Events leading to the collapse of the Tsarist regime in 1917

## THE TSAR'S LONG-TERM PROBLEMS

> Peasant poverty and land shortages led to resentment against the landowners and also to the rise of the Social Revolutionaries.

> Russia needed to industrialise quickly. She needed to provide a means of defence against modern armies like that of Germany and to provide employment for landless peasants in the new factories.

> The pace of industrial growth became so rapid that conditions for the factory workers soon became miserable.

> The growth of towns meant that new political groups wanting political change, like the Kadets and the Social Democrats, appeared.

## THE CAUSES OF THE 1905 REVOLUTION

> Russia suffered a series of humiliating military and naval defeats in the 1904–5 war against Japan.

> There were severe shortages of essential supplies in the towns because the war disrupted the normal working of the transport system.

> The events of 'Bloody Sunday' caused deep resentment amongst the population.

## HOW DID THE TSAR SURVIVE THE 1905 REVOLUTION?

> The Tsar issued the October Manifesto setting up a duma to stop middle-class opposition.

> He ended the war with Japan so that conditions became easier for workers and their protests were reduced.

> He used troops returning from the war, and Tsarist gangs, the Black Hundreds, to put down any opposition.

> In 1906, he passed two laws that reduced the power of the duma.

## The fall of the Tsar in March 1917

The First World War played a crucial part in the fall of the Tsar. Russia's shattering defeats, and the enormous loss of life among her soldiers, were blamed on the Tsar, who had made himself Commander-in-Chief in 1915. The Tsar lost the confidence and the support of the army. The middle classes were disgusted by the defeats and by the incompetence of the Tsarina. The behaviour and influence of Rasputin made things worse. The workers were tired of the shortages and angry at the enormous price rises that threatened them with starvation.

With few supporters left, the Tsar was easily overthrown. In March 1917, the bread rioters in Petrograd were joined by strikers. Many soldiers joined the rioters while the police refused to intervene. The Tsar was forced to abdicate when he realised that he no longer had any support.

Two new 'governments' were now set up:

> the Provisional Government;

> the Petrograd Soviet.

# The Provisional Government and the Bolsheviks

## Provisional Government and soviets

After the fall of the Tsar, there were two separate 'governments' that could claim the right to rule Russia: the Provisional Government, and the workers' soviets, now set up both in the countryside and in every major city. The Petrograd Soviet was particularly powerful. The middle-class Provisional Government had few supporters but the soviets, which represented the workers, peasants and soldiers, were content to allow them to rule for the time being. This was partly because the Provisional Government had announced that a Constituent Assembly (or parliament), which many people had long hoped for, would be elected later in 1917. The Bolsheviks and the Mensheviks in the soviets also believed that Russia was not yet ready for a workers' take-over. They were influenced by the ideas of Karl Marx who said that all societies went through three stages of development. The first was a feudal stage, when people were ruled over by monarchs and nobles; the second a capitalist stage, when the middle classes controlled society and developed modern industries; and the third a communist stage, when the workers would take all power for themselves. They believed that Russia had just come out of the feudal stage under the Tsar. The country now needed a period of capitalism so that the middle class could develop Russia's backward economy. Only then would the country be ready for a future communist revolution.

## Lenin and the July Days

Lenin had arrived back from exile in April 1917. At the time, it looked extremely unlikely that the Bolsheviks would seize power. Many Bolsheviks were happy to co-operate with the Provisional Government. Lenin surprised his colleagues by demanding that the Bolsheviks should stop supporting the Provisional Government and begin to organise a workers' revolution. He published his ideas in a pamphlet known as the 'April Theses'. His slogan was 'All power to the soviets'. Lenin's view was supported by Trotsky, after his return in May, but was opposed by many Bolsheviks. In July, a disorderly, armed mob, containing many disillusioned sailors and soldiers, came out on to the streets of Petrograd and tried to overthrow the Provisional Government. The plot was reluctantly supported by Lenin but it failed and he was forced to flee to Finland. These events became known as the 'July Days'. At this stage Lenin's prospects of holding power in the future looked bleak.

### Discussion point

> Why were the soviets willing to allow the Provisional Government to rule?

Troops firing on Bolshevik demonstrators in the streets of Petrograd in July 1917.

# The fate of the Provisional Government

## What caused the fall of the Provisional Government?

After the July Days, the Provisional Government seemed to have eliminated its only real opponent. A few months later, however, it was destroyed by the Bolsheviks.

### The policy of the Provisional Government

The Provisional Government made two decisions that had a particularly significant effect on future events.

---

**DECISION ONE**

The Provisional Government decided to continue the war.

The ministers in the Provisional Government believed the war could be won if it were better managed but, by the time they took over, many of the soldiers and civilians simply wanted peace at any price. The Minister of Defence, Kerensky, ordered a new military offensive to be launched in June 1917. It, too, turned into a disaster. Thousands of discontented soldiers, encouraged by Bolshevik agitators, left the front and returned home.

The decision to continue the war had important results back home as the same problems that had destroyed the Tsar continued to wear away support for the Provisional Government. Food shortages and price rises in the cities became more severe than ever. This led many disappointed people to reject Kerensky and give their support to others who promised to end the chaos and provide reliable food supplies.

---

**SOURCE A**

*Women in Petrograd queuing for food in September 1917.*

## DECISION TWO

The Provisional Government failed to introduce land reform. In the countryside, the peasants took advantage of the troubled political situation to attack the large estates belonging to the nobles. They took whatever land and property they could. Peasant leaders demanded that the Provisional Government should make these actions legal, but it refused. As a result, unrest in the countryside increased as peasants felt that they had to take the law into their own hands. The peasants continued to seize land illegally, and many thousands of soldiers at the front began to desert in order to make sure that they got their share. This, together with a series of defeats in summer 1917, hastened the break-up of the army and left the Provisional Government powerless and without support.

## Could the Provisional Government have done better?

*The war*

It would have been very difficult for the Provisional Government to withdraw from the war. It would have meant Russia letting down its allies and, in all probability, leaving them to be defeated by Germany. A triumphant Germany would then have dominated Europe. The only quick way for Russia to leave the war was to offer an unconditional surrender. The German victors were then almost certain to demand a harsh peace settlement that would take away Russia's independence and ruin the country's chances of future prosperity. A surrender would also mean that Russia would have to hand over large areas of land in eastern Europe to Germany.

*The illegal land seizures*

The Provisional Government could have recognised the illegal seizures of land made by the peasants. The members, however, claimed that, as they belonged to a temporary, unelected body, they did not have the right to make such a decision. This would have to wait until the elections of the Constituent Assembly which they decided to postpone until November 1917. Had the Provisional Government recognised the peasant gains, they would have given the go-ahead to further seizures. The countryside might have been plunged into chaos. A middle-class government which respected the law and private property could not be seen to approve of mob rule and theft.

*A painting of one of the many noblemen's houses that were looted by peasants and army deserters and then set on fire.*

## >> Activity

The Provisional Government made two critical decisions:

> to continue the war;

> to avoid land reform.

Explain in your own words the consequences of these two decisions.

# The Bolsheviks seize power

In November 1917, the Bolsheviks took control by attacking the Provisional Government's meeting place in the Winter Palace and declaring a new workers' government. The Bolshevik success was remarkable, but a number of factors make it less than surprising.

## Why were the Bolsheviks able to seize power in November 1917?

### A rise in popularity for the Bolsheviks

Lenin was in exile during the March Revolution and after the July Days, and benefited from not being associated with the failures of the Provisional Government. From the moment he arrived back in Russia, in April 1917, he demanded the overthrow of the Provisional Government with the slogan, 'All power to the soviets'. At first he was alone in making this demand. Lenin even had difficulty persuading most of the Bolshevik Party members to go along with him. As the Provisional Government became more unpopular, more people began to support Lenin's call for a revolution. The Mensheviks and Social Revolutionaries had offered their support to the Provisional Government and were, therefore, blamed for its mistakes.

### The Kornilov Plot

In September 1917, the army Commander-in-Chief, General Kornilov, attempted to move troops back from the front to Petrograd in order to destroy the soviets and arrest leading Bolsheviks. Kerensky (now prime minister) was afraid that Kornilov might be planning to take power for himself. Kerensky had no army of his own, so he was forced to arm the Bolsheviks. Trotsky was the temporary leader of the Bolsheviks as Lenin was still in hiding after the July Days. He made sure the Kornilov Plot failed by sending out Bolshevik agents to encourage Kornilov's troops to desert him. They were so successful that the Commander-in-Chief found himself with no army before he even reached Petrograd. The Bolsheviks got all the credit for stopping Kornilov. Many people had come to believe that Kerensky was really behind the plot so the other parties were made to look foolish for ever supporting him. Importantly, the Bolshevik soldiers in Petrograd (now known as the Red Guards) held on to the weapons that Kerensky had given them.

### SOURCE A

*Russian soldiers at the front, reading an illegal Bolshevik newspaper. The conditions for the demoralised front-line troops were so bad that they soon became easy targets for Bolshevik newspapers and pamphlets.*

### Peace! Bread! Land!

The Bolsheviks were the only party to offer the majority of people exactly what they wanted. They had encouraged the soldiers to desert and the peasants to seize the land that they needed. Lenin offered people 'Peace! Bread! Land!'. This slogan summed up his policies: end the war, provide food for all and bring in land reform in the countryside. It appealed to the soldiers tired of war, to hungry workers in the towns and to poverty-stricken peasants.

## Bolshevik organisation

In 1917, the Bolsheviks were a very small party, but they made up for this by their determined, professional approach. Unlike the other parties, they were well organised and they valued party unity and discipline very highly. They also made full use of very effective propaganda that soon won over many thousands to their side. By the end of 1917, the Bolsheviks were the only group with a reasonably disciplined armed force to back up their demands. This was the Red Guard of armed workers, organised and trained by Trotsky.

## The storming of the Winter Palace

After the failure of the Kornilov Plot, the Bolshevik leaders decided to take power using armed force. On 7 November 1917, Red Guards and revolutionary sailors were sent to surround and arrest the Provisional Government at the Winter Palace in Petrograd. A cruiser was sent up the River Neva and its guns trained on the Winter Palace. There was little resistance. Much of Russia was soon under Bolshevik control. Only in Moscow was there any serious fighting. After a week of conflict, the Bolsheviks had taken Moscow, and Lenin and the Bolsheviks were in power.

## >> Activity

1 Why did the Bolsheviks become more popular than the Mensheviks and the Social Revolutionaries?

2 How were the Bolsheviks helped by the Kornilov Plot?

3 What were Lenin's policies and why were they popular?

4 How did the Bolsheviks seize power in November 1917?

5 What was the most important factor that led to the Bolshevik takeover?

### INTERPRETATIONS OF THE NOVEMBER 1917 REVOLUTION

After the Bolsheviks seized power, they made every effort to make people believe that their revolution was a violent conflict during which they had heroically defeated the Provisional Government and its allies. Most historians now stress the weakness of the Provisional Government and the indifference of everyone else.

## SOURCE B

*A historian who believed that the Bolsheviks were successful simply because of the weakness of the other parties, describes the fall of the Provisional Government:*

The Provisional Government had dwindled to a meeting of ministers in the Winter Palace. It was not overthrown by a mass attack on the Winter Palace. A few Red Guards climbed in through the servants' entrance, found the Provisional Government in session and arrested the ministers in the name of the people. Six people, five of them Red Guards, were casualties of bad shooting by their own comrades.

A. J. P. Taylor, *Revolutions and Revolutionaries*, 1980

## SOURCE C

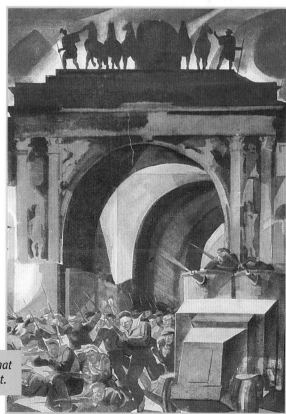

*A poster showing the storming of the Winter Palace that deliberately emphasises the heroic nature of the event.*

# The Civil War

## Origins of the Civil War

The Bolsheviks had overthrown the Provisional Government but the other political parties in the soviets, the Mensheviks and Social Revolutionaries, were angry with the Bolsheviks. They thought the overthrow of the Provisional Government was a brutal, undemocratic act. They were determined that Lenin would not hold on to power, so Lenin had to find a way to boost his support and defeat his rivals. He set about delivering his promises of 'Peace! Bread! Land!'. First of all, he handed over all lands belonging to the Church and the nobles to the peasants. He did not really like the idea of private ownership, but the measure helped reduce the opposition of the peasants to his takeover.

Next, he allowed elections to the new Constituent Assembly to go ahead because he did not dare to cancel them. The result was disappointing for the Bolsheviks. The Social Revolutionaries took most of the seats and the Bolsheviks gained only a quarter of the total number. When the Assembly met in January 1918, Lenin ordered the Red Guards to close it down after only one day. Lenin then renamed his party the Communist Party. The CHEKA, a political police force, had been set up the previous year as a means of destroying the enemies of the Revolution. Lenin now used it against his most dangerous opponents who were crushed by the use of mass executions and torture.

Some Socialist Revolutionaries and Mensheviks were willing to remain part of the soviets and voice their opposition to the Bolsheviks from within. Others fled to the outer fringes of the country where they plotted rebellion. Trotsky began to transform the Red Guards into a huge Red Army and prepare for Civil War.

## The Treaty of Brest-Litovsk

Lenin knew he had to remove the threat posed by the German troops who occupied the country. He authorised the signing of a humiliating peace treaty at the town of Brest-Litovsk in March 1918. German terms were very harsh. Russia lost one-third of its farmland and factories, a quarter of its railways, three-quarters of its iron and coal mines and 62 million of its citizens. Romania and Turkey gained Russian territory, and areas like Finland and the Ukraine fell under German influence. Lenin was willing to accept the treaty because he was certain that there would soon be a communist revolution in Germany. The treaty could then be renegotiated with the leader of the communist German government. He was also aware that much of the land that had been lost was in areas where the Bolsheviks had little support. In spite of this, many Bolsheviks disagreed with the decision to make peace. Some, like Nicolas Bukharin, wanted to continue the war in order to spread the revolution abroad and his views were widely supported in the party. Many army officers were deeply ashamed of the way Lenin had surrendered and they soon sided with the Social Revolutionaries and Mensheviks and began to recruit their own armies (known as the Whites). They planned to crush Lenin and the Reds by invading the central Bolshevik area from the fringes of the Russian Empire. Here there were a number of other nationalities, like the Georgians and the Cossacks, eager for independence and unwilling to be ruled by the Bolsheviks.

## THE TREATY OF BREST-LITOVSK, MARCH 1918

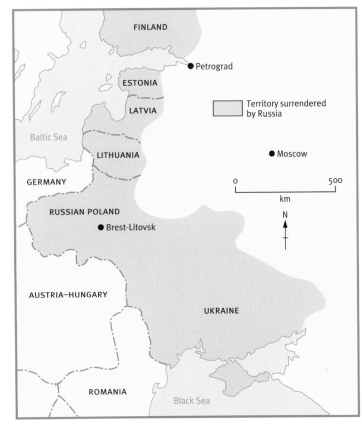

FINLAND

Petrograd

ESTONIA

LATVIA

Territory surrendered by Russia

Baltic Sea

LITHUANIA

Moscow

GERMANY

0    500

km

N

RUSSIAN POLAND

Brest-Litovsk

AUSTRIA–HUNGARY

UKRAINE

ROMANIA

Black Sea

## The Civil War

The Whites were helped by the arrival of foreign soldiers from Britain, France, the USA and Japan. Finland and Poland also attempted to take advantage of Russian weakness by choosing this time to invade the country. Facing these apparently powerful forces were Lenin's Reds. They occupied the heart of the country and the Whites attacked from different directions on the outer fringes. It was during one such White advance, in July 1918, that the Bolsheviks murdered the Tsar and his entire family, apparently out of fear that they might fall into the hands of the enemy. At first, the Reds relied on the loyal Bolshevik workers who had brought them to power to do the fighting, but there were too few of them. Soon the Whites began to take important cities and, by October 1919, even reached the suburbs of Petrograd itself. They were thrown back by a new Red Army of millions of conscripts organised by Trotsky who had become Commissar for War after the Treaty of Brest-Litovsk. One by one, the White armies were destroyed until, by March 1920, the last White soldiers only had a small toe-hold in the Crimea. In November they were forced to admit defeat and were evacuated out of the country by the British navy. The Bolsheviks were not finally in control of the country until they defeated the Georgian army in the Caucasus region in February 1921, and signed an armistice with the Poles in the following September.

## THE RUSSIAN CIVIL WAR 1918–21

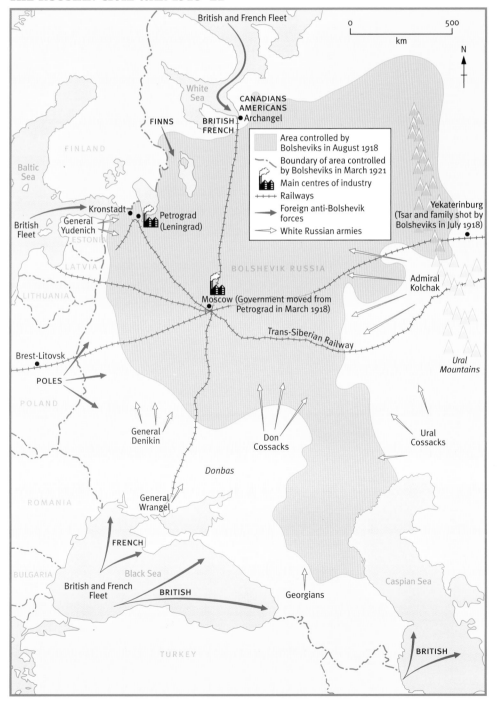

## Discussion points

> Who supported the Whites against the Bolsheviks?

> What do you think were their reasons?

# The communist victory

Although the communist position at the start of the war looked very weak compared with the Whites and their foreign allies, they had many significant advantages that made their victory always look likely.

## Why did the communists win the Civil War?

### FACTOR 1
### THERE WERE DIVISIONS AMONG THE WHITES

The Whites controlled the fringes of the Russian Empire. This was populated by many different nationalities, including the Cossacks, who only obeyed orders and co-operated with other Whites when it suited them. Lenin was able to use the presence of foreign armies on Russian soil to stir up patriotic feelings among the Russians. He portrayed the Whites as traitors who had invited the foreigners to invade Russia. Whereas the communists were one political party with a single leadership, the Whites were made up of many different political parties who constantly squabbled and did not trust each other.

### FACTOR 2
### THE REDS CONTROLLED THE CENTRAL AREA

The Reds occupied the central Russian-speaking area of the country. This made their territory easier to control. The Reds could make better use of the railway network which was centred on Moscow and needed to travel shorter distances. The scattered White armies had to travel further and found it impossible to co-ordinate their attacks.

Most of the population lived in the central area and this meant that it was easier to conscript more people into the army as they were needed. By the end of 1919, the Red soldiers outnumbered the Whites by ten to one. The Reds also controlled the most productive industrial areas around Moscow and Petrograd where arms were manufactured. The stores of the old Tsarist army and the Tsar's old arsenals, which contained 2.2 million rifles, 12,000 field guns and a plentiful supply of ammunition, fell into their hands.

**SOURCE A**

*Red Army soldiers on an armoured train during the Civil War.*

**SOURCE B**

*A Bolshevik poster demanding a 'harvest' of the White General Wrangel (on the left) and of the Poles.*

## FACTOR 3
## TROTSKY WAS AN EXCELLENT LEADER

Trotsky became Commissar for War in the new Bolshevik Government. He was a brilliant organiser and created a regular disciplined army. Despite criticisms from other Bolsheviks, he used almost 50,000 former officers of the old Tsarist army to lead the troops. Under Trotsky, the Red Army became a very effective fighting force.

## FACTOR 4
## THE RED LEADERS WERE RUTHLESS AND EFFICIENT

Lenin used his resources effectively by introducing War Communism. This system allowed the Reds total control over people's lives and possessions in order to win the war. Ruthless discipline was introduced into factories. Food was taken from peasant farmers by force. Strict food rationing was introduced, with the largest rations going to the Red Army. Lenin also used the CHEKA to terrify opponents into co-operation. Many were tortured and killed.

## FACTOR 5
## THE FOREIGN POWERS HAD NO CLEAR AIMS

The first allied troops were sent to Russia in the spring of 1917 to try to keep the war against the Germans going in the East. When the war between the allies and Germany ended, they could not really decide what to do. None of them wanted to get involved in an expensive major conflict so soon after the First World War. Although they all strongly disliked communism, they could not decide which faction of the Whites to support. Most countries sent only a small number of troops and few of these ever fought the Reds. Their most important contribution was to keep the Whites supplied with arms, ammunition and equipment. Their presence only increased support for the Reds among those who resented the foreign invaders.

## SOURCE C

*The CHEKA committed many atrocities against their opponents. It could act outside the law and did not answer to the party or to the soviets:*

The CHEKA, freed from all legal constraints, became a fearsome organ of Bolshevik power. In Kharkov, Chekists scalped their prisoners and took the skin, like gloves, off their hands. In Voronezh they placed the naked prisoner in a barrel punctured with nails and then set it in motion. In Tsaritsyn and Kamyshin they severed bones with a saw. In Poltava they impaled 18 monks and burnt at the stake peasants who rebelled. In Odessa they boiled officers and ripped them in half. In Kiev they placed them in a coffin with a decomposing corpse, buried them alive and then half-an-hour later dug them out.

Martin Macaulay, *The Soviet Union since 1917*, 1981

## SOURCE D

*An American historian describes how the foreign powers soon lost enthusiasm for the cause:*

Of the three powers most directly involved, only Britain made a serious commitment to the Whites. France lost the taste for intervention as soon as her troops were beaten in the Ukraine [in April 1919]. The United States withdrew most of her forces, leaving only those that were necessary to stop the Japanese from seizing eastern Siberia.

Richard Pipes, *Russia Under the Bolshevik Regime*, 1994

## >> Activity

Imagine you are a radio producer. Write a script for a programme entitled: Why the Bolsheviks won the Civil War. Start by making a list of all the people you would like to interview. Then decide what you think their answers to your questions would be.

# War Communism

## Why War Communism was introduced

In order to win the Civil War, the communists eventually put together an army of 3 million men. Such a huge force could only be supplied from a country whose economy was ravaged by war by taking extreme measures. Lenin, therefore, introduced a policy known as War Communism. This was a system that gave the communists direct control of all trade and industry.

## The requisition squads

The Civil War meant that few factories were actually producing goods for civilian use. With so little being made, what was available soon became very expensive, as Russia was suffering from soaring inflation. Money became almost worthless. This made the peasants very reluctant to accept money in return for their produce. The workers in the towns had few possessions that they could exchange with the peasants for food, so they soon began to go hungry. The communists responded by sending out requisition squads of soldiers led by CHEKA men to take all 'surplus' food from the peasants without payment. This ruthless policy provided some extra food for the cities, but it left the peasants very angry. The peasants then cut down the amount that they produced, so that there would be no 'surplus' for the communists to take from them. The fact that the peasants were producing less, together with two poor harvests, resulted in terrible famine in the countryside from 1921 to 1922. Around 5 million people died during this period.

## Problems in the cities

The workers in the cities were also discontented. They were forced to work longer hours under strict new laws that included the death penalty for striking. Their rations were completely inadequate, and often there were none. Some peasants brought food to barter or sell in to the cities, but the price of this black-market food was too high for most workers. Those caught trading for profit were often shot. The big cities soon began to empty as workers returned to the countryside in the hope of finding food. Petrograd lost 70 per cent of its inhabitants and Moscow lost 50 per cent during the period of War Communism. Many of those who remained moved to the extreme left of the party and became more and more opposed to the Government. They showed their feelings by joining in a number of illegal strikes in February 1921.

*A Bolshevik poster issued to encourage the requisition squads. It reads: 'You shed your blood for the workers' and peasants' revolution. The workers and peasants will deny themselves and give you their last clothes and boots. Take them!'*

*A starving family in the Volga region in 1921. Many hungry families fled from the towns, hoping to find food in the countryside, but famine soon became widespread throughout Russia.*

## Growing opposition to War Communism

By early 1921, discontent with War Communism was at its height. In the countryside, the Red Army had to put down a number of full-scale rebellions by the peasants that cost the army almost a quarter of a million lives in the space of a year. Both Trotsky and Lenin saw the dangers of War Communism. They tried to have the policy changed, but they were defeated by other leading communists who believed that, whatever the problems it caused, War Communism was necessary. The final straw came when discontent in Petrograd spread to the sailors at the Kronstadt naval base. This came as a major shock, for Kronstadt sailors were believed to be among Lenin's most loyal supporters.

Trotsky sent a Red Army force against the naval base and the revolt was crushed. Both sides, however, suffered thousands of casualties. It was now clear that Trotsky and Lenin were right. If the communists were to survive, they needed a policy to replace War Communism that would strengthen the economy and end the rising discontent in the cities and the countryside. The result was Lenin's New Economic Policy.

## Discussion point

> 'Brutal but successful.' Would you agree with this verdict on War Communism?

# The New Economic Policy

In 1921, Lenin abandoned War Communism and introduced his New Economic Policy (NEP). This reduced the government's control over the economy. Some people were allowed to work for themselves and make a profit, instead of working directly for the state. The new policy aimed to boost the economy and remove the opposition of the workers and peasants to communist rule by easing their problems.

## Was the New Economic Policy a success?

In order to persuade the peasants to grow more food, and end the widespread rebellion in the countryside, Lenin decided to put an end to the requisition squads. Instead, the government put a small tax on the food the peasants produced. This meant that the peasants began to plan to produce more, because they knew that, after they had fed themselves and paid the tax, they could sell what was left for their own profit. Lenin then allowed small-scale, private businesses to be set up outside government control to get industry and trade moving again. This return to a limited form of capitalism led to the appearance of a new class of small business men and traders, known as Nepmen.

### The benefits of NEP

In economic terms, the NEP was a real improvement on War Communism. Year by year, food production increased and industry began to recover. The value of money began to stabilise and the variety of goods on sale increased. The new policy was also a huge political success for as soon as the requisition squads stopped raiding their farms, the majority of peasants lost interest in rebellion. There were fewer strikes in the cities and no repeat of the kind of naval mutiny seen at Kronstadt in 1921.

### SOURCE B

*There were, however, some warning signs:*

Growth was rapid and so the system seemed to be succeeding beyond reasonable expectation. But this growth was based to a great extent on the re-activating of existing capacity, the re-absorption of available factory labour. Further progress would require much greater investment effort, devoted more to building new plant than repairing and renovating old ones.

Alec Nove, *An Economic History of the USSR*, 1969

### SOURCE A

The effects of War Communism and the NEP on production levels

|  |  | 1913 | 1921 | 1923 | 1925 | 1926 |
|---|---|---|---|---|---|---|
| Grain (million tonnes) |  | 80 | 37 | 57 | 73 | 77 |
| Electricity (million kWhs) |  | 1945 | 520 | 1146 | 2135 | 2441 |
| Coal (million tonnes) |  | 29 | 9 | 14 | 18 | 27 |
| Steel (million tonnes) |  | 4 | 0.2 | 0.7 | 2 | 3 |
| Average wage (per month in roubles) |  | 30.5 | 12 | 16 | 21 | 29 |

## The dangers of NEP

Although the NEP reduced discontent amongst the workers and peasants, it also posed two great dangers to Lenin's government.

### DANGER 1
### THE LEFT WITHIN THE COMMUNIST PARTY

Many communists saw the NEP as the return of capitalism and the betrayal of communist ideals and jokingly called it 'The New Exploitation of the Proletariat'. Lenin had to convince them that this was not so. He argued that the NEP was only a temporary measure to get the country back on its feet. His slogan became 'Two steps forward, one step back'. He pointed out that the government kept control of all the major industries such as power and transport, which he called the 'commanding heights' of the economy. Not all party members were convinced. In order to silence them, Lenin introduced a ban on all organised factions within the party. He intended this to be temporary, but the use of such action against fellow communists set a dangerous example for the future.

### DANGER 2
### THE RETURN OF CAPITALISM

Lenin believed that he needed to allow a limited amount of private industry to restore the country's wealth and strengthen his position. He was afraid, however, that if capitalism were allowed back, it might encourage the growth of a new capitalist political opposition that would threaten the Bolsheviks. He was determined that his party should keep total power. During this period of economic freedom, he made sure that all political freedom was severely restricted. He gave the CHEKA even more powers so that they became as feared as the old Tsarist police. A new network of labour camps for political dissidents began to open in remote parts of the country. In 1924, the country was formally renamed the Soviet Union.

**SOURCE C**

*A cartoon, published in 1924, called 'Kamenev stops the NEP Sledge'. Kamenev was a prominent communist who opposed the NEP.*
> *What do you think the artist is trying to say about those who ride the NEP sledge?*

## SOURCE D

*In 1992, a Bolshevik, Nikolai Izatchik, remembered the introduction of the NEP:*

There wasn't a scrap of food in the country. We were down to our last small piece of bread per person, then suddenly they announced the NEP. Cafés started opening, restaurants, factories went back into private hands; it was capitalism. The papers kept quoting Lenin – 'Two steps forward, one step back'; that's all very well but in my eyes what was happening was what I'd struggled against. I can remember the years 1921 and 1922; we used to discuss the NEP for hours on end at party meetings. Most people supported Lenin, others said he was wrong, many tore up their party cards.

## >> Activity

1  Was the NEP an economic success?

2  Why did some communists dislike the NEP?

3  Lenin had to persuade his party to accept the NEP. Write a speech for him, outlining the need for change. Explain how the NEP would improve the situation without letting capitalism re-emerge.

## SOURCE E

*Nepmen at a busy outdoor market in Moscow in 1921.*

# How the Bolsheviks gained control

## Why did the Provisional Government become unpopular?

The Provisional Government refused to end the war and so was blamed for the hardships that resulted. The government also refused to legalise peasant land seizures. These led to the disintegration of the army, as soldiers came home to claim their share.

After the Kornilov Plot failed, the Bolsheviks gained all the credit for this. They also had many other advantages. Their propaganda was superior. Lenin's slogan 'Peace! Bread! Land!' promised people just what they wanted. They were better organised and emphasised party loyalty. The Red Guard was the only reliable military group in Petrograd, and Lenin and Trotsky proved to be decisive leaders.

## The Civil War

The Civil War broke out because the seizure of power by the Bolsheviks, and the closure of the Constituent Assembly in January 1918, angered the other parties. Also, many patriotic Russians were ashamed when the Bolsheviks signed the Treaty of Brest-Litovsk in 1918.

The Reds had many advantages because they controlled the centre of the country. This contained most of the population, therefore it was possible to recruit a bigger army. Moscow was at the heart of the railway system which made communications easier. The Reds also inherited the Tsar's arsenal of weapons. Most people of the central area were Russian so the Reds could appeal to patriotic feelings.

The communists deserve some credit for their success. Their leadership was highly effective; the CHEKA ran a ruthless campaign of terror; the Red Army was efficiently organised by Trotsky; and an effective propaganda campaign portrayed the Whites as Tsarists.

## WAR COMMUNISM

### The results

> The peasants fought with communist requisition squads in a virtual civil war.

> Less food was grown which meant terrible famine in the countryside in 1921 and 1922.

> Food shortages in the towns led to strikes and unrest. The population in the cities left to find food in the countryside. Industry shrank and money became valueless due to inflation.

> Sailors mutinied at Kronstadt in 1921.

## THE NEW ECONOMIC POLICY

### Results of the NEP

> The requisition squads were withdrawn and instead peasants were allowed to keep their surplus and pay a small tax to the government.

> In the towns, small-scale, private industry was allowed but big businesses were kept under government control. Production increased and a new small capitalist class of Nepmen appeared.

> Opposition to the communists ended.

### Criticism of the NEP

> The new policy only restored industry and agriculture to pre-war levels of production.

> Many communists resented the NEP because they thought it represented the return of capitalism.

# Trotsky and Stalin

Lenin died of a stroke in 1924. After his death, a committee of seven – known as the Politburo – ruled the Soviet Union. It seemed likely, however, that a single leader would soon emerge. Trotsky seemed to be the most likely candidate but, over a number of years, Stalin managed to work his way up until it was he who held supreme power.

## Trotsky

Trotsky returned to Russia after the March 1917 Revolution, when the Provisional Government was in power. In the past, he had been mostly linked with the Mensheviks but, in August 1917, he was persuaded (probably by Lenin) to join the Bolsheviks. He and Lenin worked together to take the revolution further. He played an important part in the defeat of the Kornilov Plot and masterminded the military arrangements for the November 1917 Revolution. He also led the Bolshevik team that negotiated the Treaty of Brest-Litovsk with Germany. As Commissar for War, he created the Red Army and then led it to victory in the Civil War.

After Lenin's death, his rivals feared that he might use the army to overthrow the Politburo and set himself up as a dictator. Even without the support of the army, Trotsky could not be ignored; he was a powerful speaker, a talented writer and a highly original thinker.

## Stalin

Stalin became a Bolshevik after the 1903 split in the Social Democratic Party. He came from the distant province of Georgia and was viewed as an outsider by the party intellectuals from Petrograd. Although he became a leading Bolshevik from 1912 onwards, his experience was generally gained far away from the exciting events taking place in Petrograd or Moscow. During the 1905 revolution, he was the leader of a group of fighters in the remote Caucasus Mountains. As Stalin was a Georgian, Lenin at first thought of him as an expert on the problems connected with Russia's nationalities, many of whom wanted some degree of independence. He played an obscure part in the November 1917 Revolution, and became an undistinguished army commander in the Civil War.

In 1922, Stalin was elected to the position of General Secretary of the Communist Party. This entitled him to a place on the Politburo. He probably only gained the post because others viewed it as uninteresting and unimportant. Despite his Politburo place, he was a poor speaker and unoriginal thinker. Few thought that he could lead the party. He was an excellent administrator, but this seemed to make him more suitable for supporting roles in government rather than for leadership. He had no charisma and inspired no one. His colleagues called him 'Comrade Filing-Card' or the 'Grey Blur'.

## Discussion point

> Compare the roles of Trotsky and Stalin in the 1905 and 1917 Revolutions and in the Civil War.

A photo-montage, made in 1920, of the leaders of the revolution. Lenin and Trotsky appear together in the centre of the picture. Stalin's photograph has not been included.

# The rise of Stalin

After the death of Lenin, it seemed obvious that Trotsky would be the next leader of the Soviet Union. In fact, it was his rival, Stalin, who achieved supreme power.

## Why was Stalin able to defeat Trotsky?

### Suspicions of Trotsky

The fact that Trotsky was so able and had played such a glorious part in the Revolution and Civil War made other leading communists suspicious and even jealous of him. They saw him as a possible dictator, so they became determined to stop him becoming leader. Stalin's undistinguished record and his lack of charisma seemed to make him an ideal ally for those who opposed Trotsky. Trotsky's enemies completely under-estimated Stalin's own ambition and this worked in his favour.

### Stalin as General Secretary

As Commissar for War, Trotsky could have used the army to take power, but he refused to do this. Nevertheless, the very fact that he held such a powerful post made him feared and hated by the rest of the Politburo. No one else in the Politburo wanted Stalin's job as General Secretary of the Communist Party and so, unlike Trotsky, he attracted little fear or jealousy. Stalin used his position to appoint more junior party officials who supported him. These junior officials elected the Politburo itself. By promoting his friends he gained their votes and was therefore able to control the Politburo.

**SOURCE A**

*Stalin at his desk.*

**SOURCE B**

*A German cartoon showing Stalin, Zinoviev and Kamenev struggling to hold back Trotsky.*

**SOURCE C**

*In 1992, Leonid Orlovsky, a Red Army officer, commented on the leading communists' attitude to Trotsky:*

More than anything we were frightened of Trotsky seizing power, though we now know that was not the main problem. In those days Stalin was an unknown figure to us. I worked in the Kremlin [Parliament building] and I didn't know who Stalin was, and I was a Red Commander.

**SOURCE D**

*An anti-communist exile, living in the USA, describes Stalin from the point of view of someone who worked for him:*

Stalin's secretary relates that he had the habit of walking up and down his office, puffing on his pipe, then buzzing for his assistant to give a sharp command: remove such-and-such a secretary of a provincial committee and replace him with so-and-so.

Anton Antonov-Ovseyenko, *The Time of Stalin*, 1980

## The contrast between Stalin and Trotsky

Trotsky's political ideas were highly original, and this fact also worked against him. Because he created his own policies, he had to uphold them, no matter how unpopular they made him. An example of one such policy was the idea of Permanent Revolution. This would mean the Soviet Union actively helping communists in other countries to overthrow their own governments while continuing the revolution in Russia. Many party members were persuaded by their experiences in the Civil War that this policy had little chance of success. They also knew that several communist revolutions elsewhere in Europe had already come to nothing. Party members also believed that this policy might encourage capitalist countries to attack the Soviet Union itself. Many now preferred to stay out of foreign plots and concentrate on rebuilding their own country. Stalin realised that any policy which met the people's wish for peace and a stable future would be popular. In 1924, he announced his own policies. He said that the Soviet Union should isolate itself from its hostile capitalist neighbours so as not to provoke an attack. This policy became known as 'Socialism in one country'.

The fact that Stalin did not feel closely attached to any policy meant that he could change his opinions when it was to his advantage to do so. He began by supporting the extension of the NEP, with the help of Bukharin, as this meant he could isolate his opponents on the Politburo on the left of the party who were against the policy. Later he was to condemn the NEP in order to come closer to his goal of getting power. Unlike Trotsky, he was willing to change his policies in order to win popularity and make allies within the Politburo.

### SOURCE F

*Stalin's policies were popular among Bolshevik officials:*

Stalin won his battle in the 1920s to a large extent because political judgements were made in his favour among Bolshevik Party officials and not only because he controlled the levers of bureaucratic authority. Many of Stalin's inclinations were shared by many Bolsheviks.

Robert Service, *Stalin before Stalinism*, 1988

### SOURCE E

*Lenin arriving in Petrograd in 1917, at the start of the revolution. Stalin was not there at the time but, at a later date, he ordered that he should be painted into the picture. He now appears standing behind the figure of Lenin.*

## Lenin's attitude to Stalin

Just before his death, Lenin had a number of serious disagreements with Stalin. Lenin was angry at Stalin's brutal methods while in charge of putting down rebellious nationalities. When Stalin became General Secretary, Lenin was furious at the way he handed out jobs to his supporters. Lenin's will or Testament was read out at the Politburo, shortly after his death, and it demanded Stalin's complete removal from power. In spite of this, Stalin managed to survive. This was simply because many other Politburo members viewed him as a useful ally against Trotsky. The will was hushed up, and Stalin later won popularity by pretending that he had been Lenin's most trusted comrade. It now seems clear that Lenin would have preferred Trotsky to be his successor.

### SOURCE G

*Lenin's opinion of Stalin was stated in his Testament that he left to be read after his death:*

Stalin is too rude and, although we communists might put up with this, it is hardly the quality that we would expect in a General Secretary of the party. That is why I suggest he be removed from his post.

### SOURCE H

## Stalin removes his rivals

Stalin was able to force Trotsky to resign his post as Commissar for War in 1925. In 1927, he had him expelled from the party and, in 1929, had him thrown out of the country. Trotsky went into exile in a number of different countries. He moved around constantly, in order to avoid assassination by one of Stalin's agents. In 1940, he was murdered in Mexico. Once he had destroyed Trotsky's power, Stalin set about attacking his other rivals like Zinoviev, Kamenev and Bukharin. One by one, they were removed from the Politburo. By 1929, Stalin had ensured that five of the six other men with whom he had shared power in 1924 had been driven out of the Politburo.

## >> Activity

1 Why were some communists suspicious of Trotsky?

2 How did Stalin use his power as General Secretary to strengthen his position?

3 What was Lenin's view of Stalin?

4 Why was Stalin more successful than Trotsky after 1924?

Stalin with colleagues at the 1930 Communist Party Conference. He was now confident that he had removed most of those who were a threat to him from positions of power within the party.

# Collectivisation

In 1929, Stalin decided that the economic freedoms of the NEP should be abandoned. The state would at once take direct control over every aspect of economic life. He introduced a programme of collectivisation in agriculture. This meant that the thousands of small privately owned farms would be combined into a smaller number of large collective farms run directly by the state.

## Why did Stalin introduce collectivisation?

### SOVIET AGRICULTURE IN THE 1920S

Before the Revolution agriculture was highly inefficient. Farmers made little use of agricultural machinery and any new scientific methods. During the Revolution, the peasants had taken over land belonging to the nobles. While the policy of War Communism was in operation, the government tried to requisition food from these peasant farmers. This was a disastrous failure. Lenin finally gave way and allowed peasant farmers to produce food for the market under the NEP. The NEP allowed them to sell their surplus produce at a profit, so some of the peasants prospered throughout the 1920s. This led to a growth in the class of better-off peasants, known as kulaks. Although most kulaks were not really rich, they had slightly bigger farms, or a few more animals than their neighbours. They might even be able to employ other peasants during busy times of the year. This made many of the poorer peasants very jealous. Lenin wanted peasants to abandon their farms and work on large co-operative farms. However, at the time of his death, he still thought that it would not be possible to 'collectivise' the land: that is, to force peasants to work on these large co-operative farms.

### Stalin's motives

Stalin believed that bigger farms would mean that machinery could be used more effectively. Production would also increase, once advanced farming techniques were introduced on these large collective farms. He knew that it would be easier for the state to manage fewer large farms than many thousands of small ones. It would also be difficult for the peasants to hide any of their produce when they were directly supervised by communist officials. These officials would be able to estimate production levels and take the maximum possible in surplus produce from the collective farms.

Stalin knew that efficient agriculture was politically important. He felt that the failure to feed the population in the towns had led to the collapse of both the Tsar and the Provisional Government. He was determined that the same thing would not happen to his regime. In 1928, it was announced that agriculture was producing 2 million tonnes less food than was necessary to feed the city workers. He decided that drastic change was needed if he was to hold on to power.

Stalin's ultimate aim was to turn the Soviet Union into a modern industrial power but, despite the success of the NEP, industry remained limited and backward. He knew that agriculture must become more efficient before industry could safely be expanded. If industry did take off, many peasants would leave the countryside to work in factories. This would mean that there would be many more factory workers to be fed from the work of even fewer peasants working on the land.

Stalin did not trust the peasants, and saw them as natural enemies of communism. He was aware of how close they had come to destroying Lenin during the time of War Communism. He believed that, by taking away the independence they had gained from their ownership of the land, he could remove any threat once and for all. Since he could not take on all the peasants at once, he decided to destroy the kulaks first, as a warning to the others.

## SOURCE A

Peasants queuing up to join a collective farm.

## SOURCE C

*In November 1929 Stalin explained his new policy of collectivisation:*

A radical change is taking place in the development of our agriculture from small, backward, individual farming. We are advancing full steam ahead along the path of industrialisation to Socialism, leaving behind the age-long 'Russian' backwardness. We are becoming a country of metal, a country of cars, a country of tractors, and when we have put the USSR in a car, and a peasant on a tractor, let the capitalists try to overtake us.

## SOURCE B

A poster, issued in 1930, advertising the role of the Machine Tractor Stations that provided tractors and drivers for the collective farms.

## SOURCE D

*In 1994, the Soviet writer, Lyudmila Saraskina, wrote of the changes Stalin made in agriculture:*

If you imagine that Stalin wanted to improve the harvest or the lot of the peasant, then you are just fooling yourself. Collectivisation was a bloody, terrible and monstrous means of the seizure of absolute power because the free peasant and the master of the land, the farmer, constituted one of the main obstacles on the path to absolute feudal power that Stalin really wanted.

### Stalin destroys the kulaks

In the winter of 1929–30 the policy of collectivisation began. Stalin ordered that 25 million peasant farms should be combined to form 240,000 collective farms. This was a huge undertaking, involving 120 million people. Many of the wealthier peasants resented becoming unpaid workers for the state, so when the policy of collectivisation got under way they were determined to oppose it. Peasants resisted by killing their own livestock. In the first two months of 1930, 14 million cattle were slaughtered. Resistance was particularly strong in the Soviet Ukraine.

## SOURCE E

*A popular communist author describes in a novel what happened in one village:*

Men began killing their cattle every night. As soon as it was dark, you could hear the muffled bleating of a sheep, the death squeal of a pig, the whimper of a calf. In two nights half the animals in the village were killed. Cellars and barns were filled with meat. People said, 'kill, it's not ours anymore; kill, they'll take it away from you; kill, you won't get meat on the collective farm'.

Mikhail Shokolov, *Virgin Soil Upturned*, 1935

## SOURCE F

*A poster praising the work of the collective farm. It states: 'We shall carry out the grain collection plan'. In the bottom right-hand corner, angry workers corner a kulak accused of hoarding grain. The caption reads: 'Force the kulak to hand over the harvest'.*

Stalin responded with brutality. Soldiers went into the countryside where they shot anyone thought guilty of resisting collectivisation. Poor peasants who were jealous of the wealthier ones were encouraged to denounce them as kulaks. The kulaks suffered worst of all. Those peasants who had no land had nothing to lose by collectivisation, but the kulaks saw everything they had worked for taken away. Worse was to come. Stalin, not content with collectivisation alone, wanted to destroy the kulaks completely in order to show all other peasants that resistance would not be tolerated. Anyone accused of being a kulak could be imprisoned, shot, or transported to the most inhospitable parts of the country, where they would find it almost impossible to make a living. Probably around 1.5 million people were transported, usually in families, sometimes in whole villages. Many of these were to die of cold, hunger and disease. Most of the peasants who resisted had been killed or transported by 1932. By the end of 1934, 70 per cent of all land had been collectivised.

**SOURCE G**

*The bodies of victims of starvation lie abandoned in the streets of Kharkov in the Ukraine.*

The destruction of livestock had a disastrous impact on food stocks. It is estimated that in three years the farm animal population of the Soviet Union fell by around half. The combination of this destruction and the disruption caused by collectivisation led to a terrible famine in which an estimated 6 million people died between 1931 and 1933.

The production levels on Soviet farms increased after a few years, but the peasants on the collective farms did not benefit. They remained one of the poorest sections of society. They lost any power they might have had to oppose the will of the government, as Stalin had intended.

**SOURCE H**

**Grain, cattle and pigs in the Soviet Union**

|  | 1928 | 1933 | 1940 |
|---|---|---|---|
| | Figures in millions | | |
| Grain (tonnes) | 73 | 69 | 95 |
| Cattle | 29 | 19 | 28 |
| Pigs | 19 | 10 | 27 |

**SOURCE I**

*In 1933, Olya Tereschenkova, a Ukrainian peasant, left her child at home while she went looking for food. When she returned home she could not find him. There were a number of incidents such as this, where people were killed and eaten by their starving neighbours.*

I went looking for him everywhere. I ran around for two days. Then in the garden, in my neighbour's garden, I found his little head. Nobody said anything or did anything. I went off to the village soviet, they said there was nothing they could do – nothing.

>> **Activity**

1 What was the impact on Russian agriculture of:
   > War Communism;
   > the NEP?

2 Explain why Stalin might be pleased with the results of collectivisation.

3 Who would you blame for the famine of 1931 to 1933?

# The Five-Year Plans

In 1928, GOSPLAN, the agency responsible for planning the Soviet economy, produced its first Five-Year Plan. In this plan, the agency set production targets that had to be met in every area of the economy within five years. Workers in each industry, whether they were making matches or building ships, were told exactly how much they had to produce.

## Why did Stalin introduce the Five-Year Plans?

Stalin believed that the Five-Year Plans were the only way to transform the Soviet Union into an industrial power in a short space of time. He thought that the surrounding capitalist countries might attack at any moment. Only a strong industrial economy could produce the wealth and modern weapons that would be needed if the Soviet Union was to survive the coming struggle.

### SOURCE A

*Stalin stated in a speech he made in February 1931:*

To slow down the Five-Year Plan would mean falling behind. And those who fall behind get beaten. But we do not want to be beaten. No, we refuse to be beaten! In the past, Russia was beaten for her backwardness by British and French capitalists and by Japanese barons. That is why Lenin said: 'Either die, or overtake and outstrip the advanced capitalist countries'.

Stalin had other reasons for wanting to industrialise the country as quickly as possible. Communism was supposed to appeal mainly to industrial workers, yet the Soviet population was mostly made up of peasants. Stalin, therefore, thought that, if he turned the peasants into industrial workers, he would be able to broaden the support for communism among people in the Soviet Union. The power of the peasants, whom he deeply distrusted, would then be weakened. Industry could also be used to increase wealth and provide luxury consumer goods, which would keep the workers loyal to the party. Lastly, he felt that the success of the Soviet economy would impress workers around the world and increase the appeal of communism in other countries.

### SOURCE B

*A foreign capitalist laughs at the first Five-Year Plan in 1928 but, by 1933, he is silenced and shamed by Soviet progress.*

## What did the Five-Year Plans do?

There were three Five-Year Plans in the period before the Second World War. The first (1928–32) was aimed at expanding heavy industry: coal, iron, steel and oil. The second Five-Year Plan (1933–7) concentrated on making machines, particularly tractors for the new collective farms. Stalin issued regular announcements about how the Five-Year Plans were being successfully followed. Statistics were published showing amazing increases in output. Today, historians do not believe that these statistics were accurate. There is, however, no doubt that industrial output did increase dramatically. The third Five-Year Plan, which began in 1938, aimed to produce more goods such as radios and cameras for the Soviet workers. This plan had some success, but it had to be abandoned in June 1941 because of the war with Germany.

During the first Five-Year Plan, the number of industrial workers more than doubled. Whole cities were built around new industrial complexes. These were often placed in the east, in areas which were previously under-populated forest or grasslands. The choice of eastern Russia as a site for these new factories was deliberate, because it would be difficult for an enemy invading from the west to reach them. A new network of roads, railways and canals was needed to service the new industrial cities, and people were brought from all over the country to work in these new factories.

## SOURCE C

*A Soviet poster proclaiming the benefits of industrialisation: 'the chemical factory provides gas for warfare and fertiliser for farming'.*

## SOURCE D

### Official production levels during the Five-Year Plans

|  |  | 1921 | 1928 | 1933 | 1940 |
|---|---|---|---|---|---|
| Electricity (billion kWhs) |  | 0.5 | 5 | 16 | 48 |
| Crude oil (million tonnes) |  | 4 | 12 | 22 | 31 |
| Coal (million tonnes) |  | 9 | 35 | 76 | 165 |
| Steel (million tonnes) |  | 0.2 | 4 | 7 | 13 |
| Tractors (millions) |  | – | 0.1 | 7 | 3 |

The Soviet Union announced to the world that it had performed a number of amazing engineering feats: new ship canals, railways, oil fields and hydro-electric dams had been built. A new spectacular underground railway was constructed in Moscow. No expense was spared. The underground stations were luxurious, marble-lined halls that impressed visitors from all over the world.

Many of the workers were peasants, with little experience of working with machines. Industry grew so quickly that the shortage of skilled workers became a real problem. It was partly solved by bringing in foreign experts and reforming education, so that the practical subjects needed by industrial workers could be taught.

Few industries ever achieved the targets that GOSPLAN set for them. This was because the targets were much too high. Managers, who were under pressure to get results, simply lied about their progress, so many of the available statistics are likely to be inaccurate. The targets concentrated on the production of a very narrow range of goods. Many important items that were not included in the plan simply did not get made. Even the goods that were produced were often very poor. The plans always emphasised quantity and not quality.

Despite these problems, industrialisation was more successful than collectivisation. The first two Five-Year Plans turned the Soviet Union into a major industrial economy. By 1937, total industrial production was probably about four times higher than it had been in 1928. Industrialisation was often difficult, but it never faced the massive opposition from the population as a whole that had occurred during collectivisation.

## >> Activity

1 Look at the information in this unit. What reasons can you find to explain why Stalin introduced the Five-Year Plans?

2 Explain in your own words the changes that were brought about by the Five-Year Plans.

3 Why is it difficult to know how successful the Five-Year Plans were?

4 Do you think the Five-Year Plans were more or less successful than collectivisation?

# The effects of the Five-Year Plans

The far-reaching changes which the Five-Year Plans brought had a dramatic impact on the lives of every Soviet citizen, both for better and for worse.

## How did the Five-Year Plans affect the Soviet people?

### The propaganda campaign

At first, many in the Communist Party thought that it would be possible to persuade the workers to work harder by encouragement alone. A widespread propaganda campaign for the Five-Year Plans was launched through newspapers, radio broadcasts, posters, films and factory visits by party speakers. The workers were encouraged to take pride in carrying out the plan because it would make life better for everyone. It would also prove to the outside world that communism really worked. They were continually told that the country was under threat from both foreign enemies and traitors inside the Soviet Union. Only by building up industry could they hope to save themselves from invasion.

### The shock brigades and the Stakhanovites

Millions of young workers took this message seriously. They formed special teams known as 'shock brigades' whose aim was to compete with all other workers in increasing output. They were often determined communists who refused lunch breaks and worked longer hours than anyone else. They were convinced that they were building a new and better communist society and that the rest of the world would be forced to copy it when it proved successful. In 1935, a miner called Alexei Stakhanov managed to cut a record amount of coal from his coal-face. He was immediately hailed as a national hero in the press and the cinema, and was sent on a tour of the country to persuade other workers to work harder. Many others followed his example and increased their effort to set new production records in every other area of industry. These people became known as Stakhanovites. They were well rewarded for their efforts by being given extra wages, longer holidays and better housing.

So what was the cost of encouraging people to work harder? Some historians have argued that the real cost was the sacrifice of communist ideals. A key communist belief is that people should be treated equally. In order to get workers to put in an extra effort, however, Stalin had decided to give those who worked harder greater rewards than the rest. Some foreign workers were paid very good wages to come to the Soviet Union. This, too, went against the communist ideal of equality.

**SOURCE A**

*A poster celebrating the new calendar which ended the practice of taking Saints' Days as holidays. Christian, Muslim and Jewish religious figures are beaten out of the new calendar by a worker's hammer.*

**SOURCE B**

Workers studying a league table showing the production figures of rival factories.

**SOURCE C**

*Trotsky commented on the growing inequalities in the Soviet Union under Stalin:*

Qualifications, wages, employment, number of chevrons on the military uniform, are acquiring more significance, for with them are bound up questions of shoes, and fur coats, and apartments, and bathrooms, and – the ultimate dream – motor cars. The question of relatives has acquired exceptional significance. It is useful to have as a father-in law a military commander or an influential communist.

Trotsky, *The Revolution Betrayed*, 1937

**SOURCE D**

Workers' huts at the Dniepr Dam site in 1931. The living conditions of many such workers were very poor.

## How people were made to work

Many of the workers resented being told to work harder. Some people hated the Stakhanovites for continually setting higher targets which they had to follow. Some Stakhanovites were beaten up by their fellow workers and some were even murdered. It is not difficult to see why these workers disliked the Five-Year Plans. Under the first Five-Year Plan, all their hard work and the longer hours they had put in had only resulted in much poorer conditions and a lower standard of living. Few goods were being made for the workers to buy, as the government had concentrated on building up heavy industry and making machines. There was no time or material available to build houses because of the need to build factories, dams and mines. There was a real shortage of accommodation in the growing towns. For example, by 1935, only one in twenty Moscow families had more than one room to themselves. In the new towns the problem of accommodation was even worse, for the factories were always built before the homes. Workers had to live in tents, perhaps for several years. Under these conditions, it is not surprising that some workers could not be persuaded to work harder. Stalin decided that they would have to be forced.

**SOURCE E**

Newly built Moscow skyscrapers in 1950. Such buildings would house the offices or apartments of top party members.

## SOURCE F

### The production of selected consumer goods during the Five-Year Plans

| Goods (in millions) | | 1928 | 1933 | 1940 |
|---|---|---|---|---|
| Cars | | – | 1 | 0.5 |
| Cameras | | – | 3 | 35 |
| Radios | | – | 3 | 16 |
| Shoes | | 58 | 90 | 211 |

## SOURCE G

*A striking weaver commented to a leading communist in 1929:*

For 12 years already you have drivelled and agitated and stuffed our heads. Before, you said that the factory owners were unfair to us, but the factory owners did not force us to work such long hours, and there was enough of everything in the shops. Now we work long hours and one man has to do the work which four men used to do. You are bloodsuckers, and that's not all. If you go to a shop now and want to buy something, the shops are empty, there are no shoes, no clothing, nothing the worker needs.

From 1929, strict new laws were introduced to control the workers. People could lose their jobs if they were off work due to illness for a single day. Workers had to carry special documents that gave details of all the jobs they had held and any offences they had committed in the workplace. If any worker or manager failed to meet the target set for them in the Five-Year Plan, they could be treated as criminals and dealt with by the police. Some workers tried to explain their failure by accusing others of laziness, or even of deliberately holding up production by wrecking machines. Many innocent people were accused of being saboteurs in the pay of the country's enemies. In reality, machine breakdowns and other problems were usually caused by the inexperience and ignorance of the peasant workforce. When an engineer was unable to repair a machine, he could be accused of sabotage, and given no opportunity to prove his innocence. In 1933, half the engineers in the Donbas region of the Ukraine were in prison on such charges.

## SOURCE H

*Nikita Khrushchev, in a speech made in 1956, after Stalin's death, recalls the fate of some well-known factory managers:*

Both men perished in 1937. They disappeared off the face of the earth without leaving so much as a trace. Nobody would tell me what happened to them. I don't know how many factory directors and engineers perished in the same way. In those days it was easy enough to get rid of someone you didn't like. All you had to do was submit a report denouncing him as an enemy of the people; the local party organisation would glance at your report, beat its breast in righteous indignation, and have the man taken care of.

Plainly, for most Soviet people the Five-Year Plans meant hard work, poor conditions and the loss of freedom, both inside and outside the workplace.

**SOURCE I**

*A poster highlighting the support that the state offered to working women.*

## >> Activity

The year is 1936. You are a foreign worker living in the Soviet Union and working on a new steel plant. When you arrived you were a committed communist but, having seen life here, you are beginning to have your doubts. Write a letter home to a fellow communist explaining what it is that you find:

**a** most disappointing;

**b** most rewarding about working in the Soviet Union.

# The impact of Stalin's economic policies

## WHY DID STALIN INTRODUCE COLLECTIVISATION?

> If the state controlled bigger farms, output would increase and all surplus produce would be available to the government.

> There was a growing number of industrial workers to be fed.

> Crops could be exported abroad in exchange for foreign machinery.

> The independence of anti-communist peasants could be wiped out by attacking the kulaks.

All opposition was beaten down by force. The peasants who resisted the changes were deported or killed. Many peasants destroyed their animals rather than hand them over to the state. As a result, there was widespread famine from 1931 to 1933.

## WHY DID STALIN INTRODUCE THE FIVE-YEAR PLANS?

> Stalin was worried by the threat of foreign invasion. Industry was needed to strengthen the country in case of war.

> He needed to increase the number of industrial workers, who were more likely to support a communist government than were the peasants.

> He wanted to make the workers more loyal to communism by improving their living standards.

> He hoped to frighten off foreign capitalist powers and impress foreign workers with the strength and progress of the Soviet economy.

## THE THREE FIVE-YEAR PLANS

| | Areas targeted |
|---|---|
| **Plan 1** 1928–32 | Heavy industry |
| **Plan 2** 1933–7 | Agricultural machinery, particularly tractors |
| **Plan 3** 1938 onwards | Consumer goods (abandoned in 1941 because of the Second World War) |

### Achievements of the Five-Year Plans

> The output of heavy industry increased.

> Farming was boosted by providing tractors and fertiliser.

> The series of major projects impressed the world.

### Drawbacks to the Five-Year Plans

> The targets set by the government were unrealistic and this led managers to produce false statistics.

> The government laid great stress on producing vast quantities of goods. This meant that the goods were often of very poor quality.

> The failure to set targets for all goods meant that only a small range of goods was produced.

> People were made to work harder and had to put up with terrible conditions.

> The workers became more and more unequal. Foreign workers and Stakhanovites were given better treatment than the ordinary workers.

> Because the government concentrated on expanding heavy industry, few consumer goods could be produced for the workers.

> New laws severely limited workers' rights.

> Sometimes prisoners were used as workers on difficult or dangerous projects.

# The purges

### The Kirov murder

In December 1934, Sergei Kirov was shot dead outside his Moscow office. Kirov was a well-known member of the Politburo and his murder sent a shockwave throughout the Soviet Union. A hunt for those responsible was soon under way, led by the secret police (now renamed the NKVD). The government announced that their investigation had uncovered a widespread network of plots. People were accused of conspiring to kill Kirov, Stalin and other members of the Politburo, plotting to disrupt the Soviet economy and army, and planning to back the Whites. Some were even said to have been trying to help Nazi Germany to invade the country. Between 1936 and 1938, Stalin ordered a series of show trials of these people who were accused of trying to destroy the Soviet Union.

### Who were accused?

Many of the defendants were leading Communist Party members. Almost all the 'Old Bolsheviks', who played a leading part in the overthrow of the Provisional Government in 1917, were tried, found guilty and shot, after confessing to various crimes. They included men like Zinoviev and Kamenev who were members of the Politburo. Zinoviev was blamed for Kirov's murder and accused of plotting to assassinate Stalin with the help of Trotsky. Almost a million lower-ranking party members were accused of less serious crimes and thrown out of the party. Many of these were shot or sent to labour camps.

Most of the top officers in the Red Army were accused of spying for Nazi Germany. Even Tukhachevsky, the Commander-in-Chief and a hero of the Civil War, was accused of being a traitor. The army was completely purged. Half the entire officer corps was shot. Those at the top were particularly hard hit. They included Tukhachevsky himself, all eight Admirals, fourteen out of sixteen Army Commanders and sixty out of sixty-seven Corps Commanders.

Even members of the secret police were charged with treason. In 1936, Yagoda, the Head of the NKVD, was removed from his post and eventually shot. Yezhov, his successor, only lasted two years before he, too, was probably killed. Many lower-ranking NKVD men were accused of deliberately not rounding up enough traitors and they were also executed.

Of all the leading Bolsheviks, only the exiled Trotsky survived the purges or the 'Great Terror'. He was murdered in Mexico in 1940.

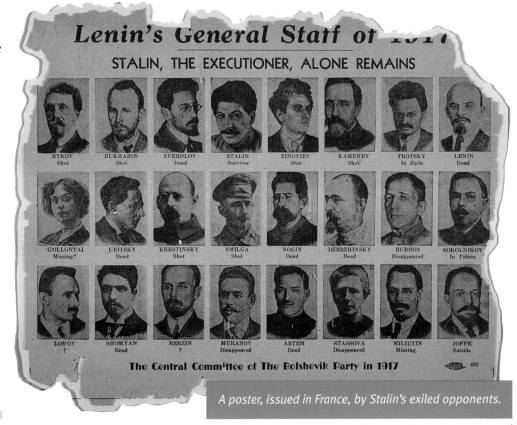

A poster, issued in France, by Stalin's exiled opponents.

### Discussion point

> What were the likely results of the purges on the security of the country and the position of Stalin?

# Threats to Stalin's power

Perhaps as many as one million people disappeared during the purges.
Only a few years before, many of the people who died had been regarded
as loyal communists or even heroes of the revolution.

## Why did Stalin launch the purges?

### The show trials

The most famous of the victims did receive a trial, but this was
merely staged for the benefit of the media, in order to justify the
purges. At these show trials, no real evidence was produced.
Instead, Vyshinsky, the Chief Prosecutor and a close ally of Stalin,
hurled abuse and false allegations at the accused. When proof was
offered, it was often found to be fabricated. In spite of this, people
almost always confessed to the most incredible crimes. Most
confessions were won by torture, starvation, deprivation of sleep
and threats against the victim's family. Some of the accused took
back their confessions in the witness stand. This led to the trial
being suspended, while the prisoners were taken away and tortured
or threatened into changing their minds.

**SOURCE A**

*Vyshinsky summing up for the prosecution at the 1936 Moscow
trial of Kamenev and Zinoviev.*

**SOURCE B**

*A mass grave in the Urals where thousands of Stalin's victims
were buried. It was opened and examined in 1989.*

## SOURCE C

A cartoon showing the common reactions of the accused at a show trial.

## SOURCE D

*In 1966, a prisoner's wife looks back, to how prisoners were interrogated:*

Until 1937, our secret police made much of their psychological methods, but afterward these gave way to physical torture with beatings of the most primitive kind; the work of undermining a person's sanity was carried on quite systematically in the Lubyanka [a Moscow prison].

The use of terror was not new in the Soviet Union. Lenin had been prepared to use violence against possible enemies of the revolution during the troubled times of the Civil War. Stalin had worked alongside Lenin during these years, and had been fully involved in the ruthless and violent way in which anti-Bolshevik forces were crushed. He had also used terror, exile and death as weapons against the kulaks during collectivisation.

There was a difference between the violence of earlier times and the purges. The victims of the earlier violence were anti-communist, while the victims of the purges were often leading communists. The purges did great damage to the Soviet Union. Thousands of talented managers and army officers were destroyed. This has led some people to suggest that Stalin was insane. Others have said that his actions were not mad, but were clearly calculated.

## STALIN: INSANE OR CALCULATING?

> Trotsky had opposed Stalin in the 1920s. He was expelled from Russia in 1929, but he remained active abroad. While in exile, Trotsky wrote many books and articles that were critical of Stalin. Trotsky had little open support in the Soviet Union, but Stalin was sure that many people secretly supported him.

> In the purges Stalin destroyed all the leading communists who had taken part in the 1917 Revolution and the Civil War. Stalin felt threatened by these people because his own part in the revolution had been undistinguished. He felt that these 'Old Bolsheviks' were loyal to the memory of Lenin, but were not loyal to him. By destroying them, he intended to create a new Stalinist Communist Party.

> Although Stalin was rapidly gaining control of the Soviet Union by 1929, he continued to feel at risk. He saw signs that many in the party did not support him. In 1932, an intellectual named Ryutin circulated a document calling for Stalin's removal from the post of General Secretary. Stalin demanded that Ryutin should be executed, but he was defeated by a vote in the Politburo. At the 1934 Party Congress, 270 delegates voted against Stalin keeping his place on the Politburo. Sergei Kirov, whom many wanted to make General Secretary in Stalin's place, received more votes than Stalin did.

SOURCE E

*Rykhov and Bukharin, two former members of the Politburo, under arrest.*

## SOURCE F

*Nikita Khrushchev became the leader of the USSR after Stalin. In 1956, three years after Stalin's death, he made a speech in which he denounced Stalin:*

Stalin was a very distrustful man, sickly suspicious; he could look at a man and say 'Why are your eyes so shifty today?' or 'Why are you turning so much today and avoiding to look me directly in the eyes?'

## SOURCE G

*In 1938, a few months before he was executed, Bukharin, another Politburo member, said privately:*

The predominant view in party circles was that Stalin had led the country into a dead-end by his policy, that he had roused the peasants against the party, and that the situation could be saved only by his removal. Many influential members of the Central Committee were of this opinion.

## Who killed Kirov?

Most historians now agree that Stalin probably had Kirov killed as a way of justifying the purges. He also got rid of a popular rival at the same time. There is evidence that Stalin wrote a special decree to punish 'those responsible' for Kirov's murder before it had even taken place. In the months after the murder, he successfully covered up his own part in events by making sure that everyone remotely connected with the case died suddenly and mysteriously.

## >> Activity

1 Explain in your own words what happened during the purges of the 1930s. In your answer you should mention:
   > Kirov;
   > the show trials;
   > the Red Army.

2 Using the whole of this unit for information, explain whether you think Stalin:
   > carried out the purges because he was insane; or
   > because he was calculating.

# Stalin gains control

The purges ended opposition to Stalin from within the higher reaches of the Communist Party.

## How did Stalin control the people of the Soviet Union?

### The cult of personality

From the mid-1930s onwards, Stalin ruthlessly used the machinery of government to show himself in a favourable light. He created an image of himself as a caring leader whose genius had saved the Soviet Union from its enemies and made it the envy of the world. This widespread propaganda campaign was directed particularly at children. School children were taught from textbooks specially written to exaggerate Stalin's importance in the revolution. They praised his successes in collectivising agriculture and building up industry. Outside school, they were encouraged to join the communist youth movement known as the Komsomol, which further indoctrinated them with Stalin's ideas.

Artists, writers and film-makers were told that they must produce works in praise of Stalin and his achievements. The propaganda campaign reached into every area of life. It became a cult of personality. Ordinary people were told that Stalin was the essence of all that was good and wise, almost a god-like being. Stalin promised to reward those who were loyal to him with better housing and promotion at work. A large group of party members (known as 'apparatchiks' because they were part of the party apparatus) could soon be seen enjoying a better lifestyle than other citizens.

### SOURCE B

*In 1936, a poem written by the Soviet poet, Audienko, shows how far the personality cult of Stalin was taken:*

O Great Stalin, O leader of peoples
You who created man.
You who makes the trees grow fruit
You who makes the flowers grow in spring
You who makes everyone happy.

### SOURCE A

*A propaganda poster showing Stalin with children.*

### The 1936 Constitution

In 1936 Stalin introduced a new constitution that appeared to give greater freedom and democracy to Soviet people. Everyone over 18-years old was allowed to vote for a new National Assembly (a new, two-chamber soviet). In theory, they were given the right to say or write whatever they wanted. Stalin claimed that the 1936 Constitution made the Soviet Union the most democratic country in the world. In reality, the rights written into the constitution were a sham. The National Assembly only met for two weeks a year, and the ruling committee of the Communist Party, headed by Stalin and packed with his followers, continued to hold complete power. The right of individual citizens to express their own ideas without fear of punishment did not exist. Stalin had no intention of allowing anyone to criticise him.

### SOURCE C

*A poster showing Stalin planning an irrigation project.*

### SOURCE D

*A painting of Stalin called 'Morning of the Motherland'.*

### The secret police

In such a large country, it was obviously difficult to identify all those who were disloyal, but Stalin had his methods. The NKVD spied on every area of life. They could arrest almost anyone and punish them on the flimsiest of evidence. Ordinary workers were encouraged to spy on each other. Anyone who criticised Stalin or his policies was likely to be reported. Soon many people discovered that the best way of avoiding arrest was to denounce someone else. In this way one could prove oneself loyal to Stalin. Betraying one's colleagues at work, or even family members to the NKVD could also lead to other worthwhile rewards. Once arrested, a person would often be brutally interrogated until they accused someone else. Thus one arrest might eventually lead to many more.

### SOURCE E

*Two historians describe life under the NKVD:*

Under Stalin the whole nation was urged to become an informer. It was a way of showing your loyalty. It became a means of settling old scores, or of taking your boss's job, or the flat of a friend; even, it was said, someone else's wife or husband. A key part of Soviet society became the moral despair forced on so many by having to lie or keep silent out of fear.

J. Lewis and P. Whitehead, *Stalin: A Time for Judgement*, 1994

## Stalin's victims

People who were accused might be arrested in the middle of the night, taken away and never seen again. Around a million people were probably taken to isolated areas and shot. Their bodies were buried in unmarked, mass graves.

Others were sent to one of a growing number of labour camps, known as gulags. These were built in the most inhospitable areas of the country. Prisoners were made to work in such terrible conditions that one in five died each year from cold, ill-treatment or hunger. As many as 12 million probably died in the gulags. One estimate puts the number of camp inmates during the 1930s at 7 or 8 million: one in twenty of the population. The system of labour camps had other advantages for Stalin. The prisoners could be forced to work on unpleasant or dangerous projects in areas where ordinary workers did not want to go. Ordinary communists were proud of these major projects, but many were only achieved through the misery and sacrifice of the gulag prisoners.

Stalin's crude system of detection and punishment may not have actually caught many of the people who genuinely opposed him. Even so, the threat of the informer, the NKVD and the gulags was enough to silence all opposition and allow him total power. The propaganda campaign convinced others that all of Stalin's actions were right.

### SOURCE F

*Gulag workers constructing the Belomor Canal. The government saved money and punished the prisoners further by not allowing them to use machinery. As many as 300,000 may have died. When the work was finished, it was discovered that the canal was incapable of taking large ships.*

### SOURCE G

*In 1967, a former manager of a collective farm remembered Stalin:*

I was in love with that man, and I love him still. The day he died I wept like a baby. I loved him for his mind, his logic, his manliness and especially his courage. He was the one person great enough to keep the Soviet Union together and make us a great nation after Lenin died. It was for him that we worked and sacrificed and died. He was a genius of his time.

### SOURCE H

*Alexander Avdeyenko, a Stakhanovite steelworker, looked back in 1990 at life under Stalin:*

It would have been impossible for a common mortal to withstand the onslaught of the apparatus which was Stalin's, or the pressure which was put on people's reason, heart and soul. Day and night radio told us that Stalin was the greatest man on earth – the greatest statesman, the father of the nation, the genius of all time; man wants to believe in something great.

## >> Activity

1 Look at Sources A–D. What impression of Stalin was each source meant to give to Soviet people?

2 Explain each of the methods used by Stalin to ensure obedience.

3 Why did people inform on each other?

4 The gulags served two purposes for Stalin. What were they?

5 Despite his monstrous crimes, Stalin was never overthrown. Use the information in this unit to explain how Stalin was able to hang on to power.

# How did Stalin win and hold on to power?

## THE CONTRAST BETWEEN STALIN AND TROTSKY

### Trotsky

> Trotsky was feared.

> Trotsky would not use his position (Commissar for War) to take power.

> Trotsky's policies (especially his theory of Permanent Revolution) were seen as dangerous.

### Stalin

> Stalin was underestimated.

> Stalin used his position (General Secretary of the Communist Party) to appoint his friends who then supported him.

> Stalin's policies (Socialism in one country) were seen as safe.

> Stalin stole Trotsky's image as Lenin's right-hand man by skilful propaganda.

## The purges

These began with the murder of Kirov. Three prominent groups were purged:

> the 'Old Bolsheviks', who were accused of plotting with Trotsky;

> the military who were accused of plotting a coup helped by the Nazis;

> the NKVD who were accused of being inefficient in purging opposition.

Most prominent people received a show trial in order to impress the ordinary citizens and the foreign media. Threats and torture were used to extract confessions.

As many as a million ordinary party members were probably purged without trial. Many were shot. Others were sent to the gulags.

## Why did Stalin start the purges?

It is difficult to be exactly sure why Stalin ordered the purges. His brutal policies towards the peasants and workers probably encouraged opposition within the party itself so that he felt he would have to deal with it. Kirov was his only rival. Stalin had him murdered, and used his death as an excuse to fabricate widespread plots and start the purges.

## HOW DID STALIN CONTROL ORDINARY PEOPLE?

### Persuasion

> A personality cult was carefully encouraged. A massive propaganda campaign was launched through the arts and the media. Stalin was portrayed in school textbooks and in the classroom as a genius who saved the Soviet Union from its enemies.

> The 1936 Constitution was adopted. Stalin tried to persuade ordinary citizens and foreigners that the Soviet Union was the most democratic country in the world. The constitution was a sham and democratic rights existed only on paper.

> Stalin made sure that those who supported him gained privileges, higher wages, promotion and better accommodation.

### Coercion

> The NKVD carried out widespread spying operations among the population. Millions of ordinary citizens were recruited to spy on each other.

> An atmosphere of terror was created by arrest and imprisonment without trial and brutal punishments. No one dared speak out against Stalin.

> Stalin ordered the setting up of a vast system of gulags where as many as 12 million people may have died.

# The Great Patriotic War

## The Nazi–Soviet Pact

On 23 August 1939, the Soviet foreign minister, Molotov, met with his German counterpart, Ribbentrop, and signed a non-aggression agreement between the two countries. This became known as the Nazi–Soviet Pact. Stalin had watched the expansion of Nazi Germany with great concern. He was convinced that, should the USSR be attacked, he could not rely on help from France or Britain. These two countries had both refused to sign a treaty with the Soviet Union. He believed that a war between Germany and Russia would come, but he hoped that he could buy valuable time to prepare by making an agreement with the Nazis. A short time after the Pact was signed, the Red Army helped the Nazis to invade Poland and, in return, was allowed to annex territory that had been lost after the Treaty of Brest-Litovsk in 1918.

## The German invasion

Less than two years later, in June 1941, Hitler decided to invade the Soviet Union. Stalin was taken completely by surprise as three enormous German armies, with support from the air, pushed into the country in a blitzkrieg attack, code-named Operation Barbarossa. Within the first few weeks of the invasion, the Germans took hundreds of thousands of prisoners, conquered a large area of territory and destroyed the Red Air Force on the ground. The Red Army had been severely weakened by the loss of so many officers in the purges. All it could do was retreat, destroying everything that might be of use to the enemy. Stalin panicked and disappeared from public view for almost two weeks after the invasion. When he eventually recovered his nerve, he made a radio broadcast. He appealed to the Soviet people to fight the invader, not for the sake of communist principles, but out of patriotism. At first, despite his appeals, many Soviet citizens actually welcomed the Nazis as liberators from Stalinist oppression. The Soviet Union looked close to collapse.

As the winter set in, the Germans were poised to take Moscow and Leningrad. The winter of 1941 was particularly severe and the Germans, who had prepared for a short campaign, suffered terribly from cold and a shortage of supplies. It was at this point that their attack ground to a halt at Leningrad (formerly Petrograd). In December, the civilians joined the Red Army to hold off the assault on their city for almost three years. At Stalingrad, late in 1942, the Germans suffered huge casualties as they fought their way forward, building by building. They never did manage to take the whole city.

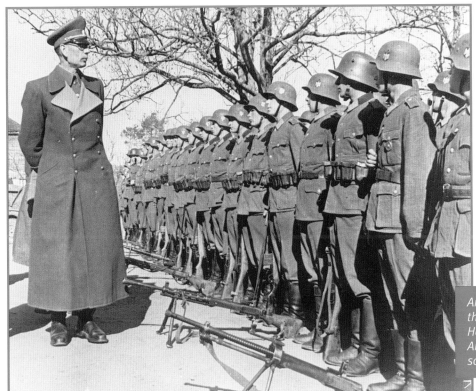

*Around a million Soviet citizens joined with the German army to fight against Stalin. Here, in 1944, their commander, General Andrei Vlasov, is inspecting a group of soldiers at the front.*

As the German attack faltered, Stalin and his new commander Marshal Zhukov were preparing a counter-stroke. The USA and Britain shipped tonnes of vital supplies to the USSR by the Arctic Sea route. Because of the Five-Year Plans, the Soviet Union was now able to supply much of its own arms and equipment. The new industrial complexes which had been set up in the east of the country were working at full capacity. They were joined by thousands more factories as machinery and workers were moved out of the war-zone by train. Soon, new armies equipped with the latest weapons had been formed in the east. They advanced westward in November 1942, sweeping around the Germans in Stalingrad and cutting off their escape route. The 91,000 German troops in the city were forced to surrender in February 1943.

The poorly supplied Germans were now no match for the Red Army. They were pushed back through Russia and Eastern Europe in a series of bitterly fought battles. In June 1944, the Western Allies landed their armies in France and the Germans were forced to fight a war on two fronts. Marshal Zhukov led the Red Army assault on Berlin in April 1945. Its capture brought an end to the war.

## THE GERMAN OFFENSIVE IN THE GREAT PATRIOTIC WAR 1941-2

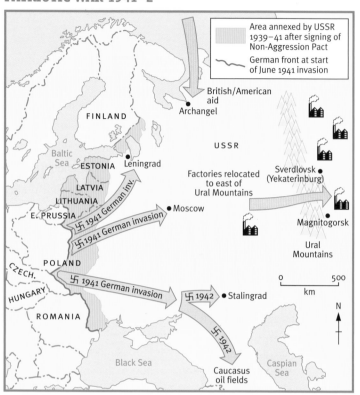

*This Soviet painting of 1948 shows Stalin personally planning the victorious counter-attack against the German armies.*

### Arms production in Germany and the Soviet Union during the Second World War

| Arms produced | | Soviet Union 1941-5 | Germany 1941-4 |
|---|---|---|---|
| Rifles | | 12,000,000 | 7,500,000 |
| Mortars | | 347,900 | 68,000 |
| Field guns | | 97,768 | 44,800 |
| Tanks | | 95,099 | 53,800 |
| Combat aircraft | | 108,028 | 78,900 |

## Discussion points

> Should Stalin have signed the Nazi–Soviet Pact?

> Why were the Germans unable to conquer the Soviet Union?

> How important a part do you think Stalin played in the victory over Germany?

# Stalin's successors

Stalin died of a brain haemorrhage in 1953. He left two major problems for those leaders who came after him. These were: how should the Soviet Union relate to its capitalist neighbours and how could the Soviet economy be run for the benefit and prosperity of the people?

## How did Stalin's successors deal with the Soviet Union's problems?

### STALIN'S LAST YEARS

The war destroyed both agriculture and industry in Russia and Stalin sought to repair the damage through a further series of Five-Year Plans. Once again, ordinary people were forced, through fear, to work harder. More purges were launched, this time against the returning prisoners of war. They were viewed as potential traitors for having surrendered to the German army.

After the war, Stalin felt threatened by the power of America and their atomic weapons first used against Japan in 1945. He was determined that the Red Army should stay in many of the countries in Eastern Europe that they had overrun at the end of the war. By intimidation and election fixing, he was able to make sure that friendly communist governments came into power in Poland, Czechoslovakia, Hungary, Romania, Bulgaria and the eastern part of Germany. He saw this as a defensive move, because he believed that they would provide a buffer zone against another attack from the West. The West, however, interpreted his actions as the start of an aggressive plan to conquer all of Europe. This led to a new period of distrust between the USSR and the West known as the Cold War.

SOURCE A

This poster, issued after the war, urges workers to rebuild the ruined city of Leningrad.

### Khrushchev's new approach (1953–64)

After Stalin's death, in March 1953, a period of collective leadership began during which it was decided to end the use of terror. Nikita Khrushchev eventually emerged as the new leader. He was determined to remain in total control and he could be brutal to opponents. In general, he wanted to rule, not by terror, but by winning support and popularity both at home and abroad. In 1956, he made an important speech denouncing Stalin's methods and pointing out the falsehoods on which his personality cult had been based.

## De-Stalinisation

This speech began a process known as 'De-Stalinisation'. Stalin's carefully built-up public image was shattered. His portraits and statues were removed from public display and history books were re-written all over the communist world to show him in a truer light. Khrushchev now began to carry out his own ideas for solving the Soviet Union's problems. Although Khrushchev could destroy Stalin's reputation, he soon found out that his own ideas were blocked by many of the old Stalinists. They held key positions in the Moscow central committees that planned the economy.

## Khrushchev's reforms

Khrushchev's main aim in agriculture was to open up new 'virgin' lands in remote regions that had never before been farmed. Almost half-a-million young volunteers were sent out to grow wheat on these new state farms. The new wheat-producing areas allowed land in established areas to be used for growing animal fodder. This ultimately meant more meat and dairy products for the whole population. He brought in a new Seven-Year Plan for industry, aimed at producing more consumer goods and luxury items for the Soviet people. He hoped to manage these improvements more efficiently by setting up a large number of regional planning groups. In this way he would by-pass his enemies on the central planning committees in Moscow.

## SOURCE B

*Some comments on Khrushchev's problems and policies:*

The Moscow-based planning bodies no longer had a firm grip on what was happening. They lacked the capacity to promote rapid technical progress. By the mid-1950s, the Soviet Union recognised its enormous technical lag behind the advanced capitalist countries. It became clear that major reform of the traditional planning mechanism was required.

In foreign policy he tried to end the Cold War by seeking 'peaceful coexistence' with the West. He hoped that this less confrontational approach would make possible a large cut in defence spending, allowing him to use the manpower and money saved elsewhere in the economy.

Ronald Amman, *The Soviet Union*, ed. R. W. Davies, 1989

## SOURCE C

*Khrushchev inspecting the crops during a tour of Soviet farms.*

## Why did Khrushchev's new approach fail?

Unlike Stalin, Khrushchev was not a planner. He was a man with imperfectly thought-out bright ideas. His Virgin Lands scheme at first went well and yielded bumper harvests, but soon its pitfalls were apparent. Many crops were planted on land with an unsuitable soil or climate. After a few harvests, the soil became exhausted or the supply of water proved completely inadequate. As a result, the amount of new land under cultivation fell dramatically.

Industry suffered from the inexperience of the new committees and from the constant opposition of the old Stalinists, who were determined to sabotage all reforms. Khrushchev refused to use force against workers and planners. This meant that they could not be threatened into producing more. By 1964, the rate of industrial production actually started to fall.

Khrushchev's foreign policy was damaged by a series of crises involving his East European allies and the West. His more liberal policy towards his own citizens encouraged eastern communist countries to try to seek greater freedom from the USSR. In 1956, he had to drop his image as a reformer and send the Red Army into Hungary to restore a hard-line communist government. In 1961, he ordered the Berlin Wall to be built to prevent people escaping from communist East Germany to the West. Relations with the USA were badly damaged in 1960, when the Soviet Air Force shot down an American spy plane over Soviet territory.

Further damage was done two years later, when the Soviet Union was forced to give up its plans to place nuclear missiles on the island of Cuba as a result of measures taken by the American President, John F. Kennedy.

By 1964, Khrushchev's policies had failed. The economy was in poor shape and defence spending had to be increased once more as relations with the West became embittered. He was forced to resign at a meeting of the Presidium (a new name of the Politburo) and retired into peaceful obscurity. After a bloodless struggle, Leonid Brezhnev became a leader.

## The Brezhnev years (1964–82)

Brezhnev realised that any attempt to reform the economy would meet with opposition from the same hard-line communists who had overthrown Khrushchev. He therefore decided to avoid major reform. Although living standards rose during his time in power, the Soviet Union's economy actually stagnated in comparison with the West. Despite the growing problems, many workers were willing to accept the stability that Brezhnev offered.

### SOURCE D

*A historian writes:*

For the factory worker, the centralised planning system means, on the whole, a poorly paid, but secure and fairly undemanding life. It is difficult for management to dismiss workers for laziness, incompetence, absenteeism or even drunkenness.

Geoffrey Hosking, *A History of the Soviet Union*, 1985

### SOURCE E

There were a small number of people, known as dissidents, who openly opposed the government. These were the writers and scientists who resented government control over their work, religious groups who were discriminated against, and the leaders of some of the nationalities who wanted greater freedom from Soviet control. The most prominent group of dissidents was the Jews who wished to leave the Soviet Union and live in Israel. Thousands were allowed to go, but many of the better educated were not allowed to leave. They were too valuable for the country to lose. This made the Soviet Union very unpopular with some people in the West. Brezhnev cracked down hard on the dissidents. Many were sacked from their jobs, imprisoned or even sent to mental hospitals.

## Brezhnev and the world

Brezhnev's foreign policy favoured peaceful co-operation with the West. In a period of improving relations known as détente, agreements were reached on sharing scientific research. Some progress was also made in limiting nuclear arms with the Strategic Arms Limitation Treaty (SALT). Brezhnev's hopes of strengthening détente were destroyed by his own ambitious policies which frightened the West. In 1968, he invaded Czechoslovakia in order to overthrow a reforming communist government. After that, the Soviet Union claimed the right to intervene in support of any communist government, anywhere in the world. Brezhnev supported these policies, known as the 'Brezhnev Doctrine', by spending more on armaments, including new nuclear missiles. The West responded with their own new weapons and soon an expensive arms race was under way. In 1979, the Soviet invasion of Afghanistan appeared to end all chances of avoiding a new Cold War. Brezhnev was now a sick old man surrounded by ageing party leaders. He died in 1982.

*Brezhnev with other ageing Soviet leaders on a visit to the Ukraine in 1981.*

## SOURCE F

*Soviet missiles on view during the 1989 Revolution Day Parade in Moscow.*

## The Gorbachev reforms

Brezhnev had been succeeded by two of his old colleagues (Andropov, a reformer who had hoped that Gorbachev would succeed him, and Chernenko) but they both died soon after taking office. In 1985, the leadership passed to a much younger man, Mikhail Gorbachev.

He now set out to confront the problems which Brezhnev had avoided. He started by demanding a policy of 'glasnost' (openness) that would allow many critics in the media and the arts to broadcast and publish their criticisms. The full extent of the incompetence and corruption of the Soviet system was now on public display. Gorbachev did not object to this. He hoped to use public anger to destroy the influence of his hard-line communist opponents and get support for his next policy, 'perestroika' (restructuring the economy). He began to pass laws to weaken the central control of the Communist Party over industry. He even encouraged the growth of small-scale private businesses in the hope that they would compete with the inefficient state enterprises.

## SOURCE H

*Mikhail Gorbachev said, in a speech made in 1986:*

Can the economy really be run by trillions of calculations from Moscow? That's absurd, comrades! And that is where the greatest mistake lies, in the fact that until very recently we have tried to run everything from Moscow.

Gorbachev adopted a third policy, 'demokratizatsiya' (democracy) that, from 1988–90, led to more powerful soviets being elected. Gorbachev's reforms created much opposition from hard-liners within the Communist Party. He realised that he needed to weaken the party strength and gain support from reformers outside the party. He, therefore, decided to allow non-communist reform groups to contest elections against official party candidates.

## SOURCE G

*President Gorbachev and President Bush at the Washington Summit in June 1990.*

## Gorbachev's foreign policy

Gorbachev moved quickly to put an end to the expensive and dangerous arms race. In a series of face-to-face meetings with American Presidents, Reagan and Bush, he agreed to real arms reductions. He also removed another cause of friction with the West by pulling Soviet troops out of Afghanistan. In the countries of Eastern Europe the communist governments were overthrown by reformers. Gorbachev refused to intervene.

## The end of the Soviet Union

The reforms now ran into trouble. Economic difficulties were creating hardship for most ordinary people and many of the Soviet Union's nationalities were demanding independence as a means of solving their problems. Gorbachev was caught between the hard-line communists who demanded an end to all reform and the reformers led by Boris Yeltsin who said that the reforms had not gone far enough. Gorbachev tried to deal with the problem of the nationalities by ending the strong central power of the Soviet system. He planned to replace it with a loose-knit Confederation of Independent States.

### SOURCE I

*Yeltsin rallies his supporters from a tank near the Russian Federation Building after the failure of the coup against Gorbachev in 1991.*

This was the final straw for the hard-liners. They had seen the power of their party weakened, and Soviet influence in Eastern Europe destroyed. Now they were being asked to stand by and witness the destruction of the Soviet Union itself.

In August 1991, they attempted to take power in a coup. Gorbachev was arrested, and it was only the action of the reformers led by Yeltsin that defeated the plotters.

Gorbachev now had little choice but to obey the demands of the reformers. The Communist Party was outlawed and, in December 1991, the Soviet Union was replaced by the Commonwealth of Independent States (CIS) that incorporated 11 out of the 15 republics of the USSR. Gorbachev then resigned and Boris Yeltsin remained in power as President of the Russian Federation, the largest state in the CIS.

## >> Activity

1 Explain the following:
   > de-Stalinisation;
   > détente;
   > glasnost;
   > perestroika;
   > CIS.

2 Compare the policies of Krushchev, Brezhnev and Gorbachev in the following areas:
   **a** relations with the West;
   **b** relations with Eastern Europe;
   **c** planning the economy.
   Which two leaders were most alike in their policies?

3 Explain the role of communist hard-liners during the leadership of Khrushchev, Brezhnev and Gorbachev.

4 Explain how Gorbachev hoped glasnost would help bring in perestroika.

5 Why might the workers in Source D feel threatened by Gorbachev's statement in Source H?

# The Soviet Union after 1941

## THE GREAT PATRIOTIC WAR

### Why Germany was defeated

> The German troops were drawn further and further into the USSR by the retreating Red armies and their lines of communications became over-extended.

> The German troops became bogged down in the autumn of 1941 and soon found that they were not equipped for the extreme cold of the Russian winter.

> The Germans were short of food, equipment and fuel.

> The Soviet people showed extreme determination, for example, to survive the siege of Leningrad and to defend the city of Stalingrad.

> Britain and the USA shipped vital supplies to the USSR by the Arctic sea route.

> The industrial complexes in the east of the country were working well by 1942, and were out of reach of German attacks.

> From late 1942, new Soviet armies, equipped in the east, pushed the weakened German troops westward and also cut off the German forces at Stalingrad. The Soviet troops continued to advance until Berlin was captured in April 1945.

## KHRUSHCHEV'S NEW APPROACH (1953–64)

> Stalin's policy was denounced.

> New areas of land were opened up for agriculture.

> A new Seven-Year Plan was introduced to produce more consumer goods.

> A policy of peaceful coexistence with the West was attempted.

### Why did this fail?

> Krushchev's new ideas were often not fully thought out.

> Much of the new land was not suitable for cultivation.

> The old Stalinists continuously opposed his ideas.

> A series of crises upset relations with the West.

## BREZHNEV'S POLICY (1964–82)

> Brezhnev avoided major economic reform so living standards rose but the economy stagnated.

> He cracked down on dissidents within the Soviet Union.

> Although he favoured peaceful co-operation with the West, his crushing of democracy in Czechoslovakia and arms spending provoked an arms race.

## GORBACHEV'S ATTEMPTS AT REFORM (1985–91)

> He promoted a policy of glasnost within Soviet society.

> He tried to restructure the economy by his policy of perestroika.

> He worked towards ending the arms race and improving relations with the West.

### What problems did he face?

> On the one hand, the hard-liners opposed his policies while, on the other, reformers, led by Yeltsin, began to demand even more changes.

> The economic reforms caused hardship amongst the Soviet people.

> Many of the nationalities began to use their new freedom to demand independence from the USSR.

### The CIS

In August 1991, the hard-liners tried to overthrow Gorbachev's government but reformers, led by Boris Yeltsin, rallied to his support. In December 1991, the CIS replaced the USSR and Yeltsin became President of the Russian Federation.

# Index